Understanding
Phobias

GEDDES&
GROSSET

This edition published 2000 by Geddes & Grosset,
an imprint of Children's Leisure Products Limited

© 2000 Children's Leisure Products Limited,
David Dale House, New Lanark, ML11 9DJ Scotland.

Cover picture courtesy of PhotoDisc, Inc.

ISBN 185534 938 8

Printed and bound in Europe

Contents

Chapter 1
Phobias

Introduction and general definition

A phobia is an anxiety disorder characterised by an overwhelming fear or dread of certain objects, animals, events or situations. A phobia can cause severe disruption and restriction of normal life activities and, at its worst, intense misery and suffering for the phobic person. The word is derived from the Greek *phobos* meaning extreme fear and flight. The ancient Greek god, Phobos, was believed to be able to reduce the enemies of the Greeks to a state of abject terror, making victory in battle more likely.

It is precisely this sort of incapacitating fear which grips the phobic person when confronted by the phobia stimulus and sometimes, even the anticipation or thought of the situation is enough to provoke the response. The fear is so strong that it produces a range of physical symptoms which typically may include sweating, trembling, feelings of faintness and dizziness, nausea, palpitations, hyperventilation and panic attack (*see* page 15). There are, however, some apparent differences between the various categories of phobia, particularly with regard to their development, and these are discussed in more detail in Chapter 21.

A phobic person recognises that his or her fear is irrational and completely out of proportion to any possible threat posed by the stimulus and this, in itself, can be the cause of feelings of intense embarrassment. A person may go to great lengths to conceal the existence of his or her phobia and it is probable that, in many cases, the disorder remains unrecognised. This is especially likely when it is appreciated that there remains a lingering attitude, even in the modern Britain of today, that any form of mental disorder is a subject of shame.

The present situation

Recent surveys have revealed that phobias, especially specific ones, are the most commonly diagnosed mental disorder in Western psychiatric medicine. Studies indicate that between ten and thirteen per cent of the population may be affected at any one time with non-diagnosis making the figure even higher. Children and adults of both sexes are affected and an untreated child may or may not carry the phobia into adult life. Some people have a single phobia while others are phobic in response to several or many stimuli. Age and gender are sometimes relevant with certain phobias being more common to a particular age or sex.

Phobia occurs at the extreme end of a sliding scale which passes down through unreasonable, but less crippling fear, to aversion and strong dislike. If these responses are taken into consideration, most people would probably admit that they have experienced phobic symptoms to a certain extent, even if only on a single occasion. In fact, surveys have shown that sixty per cent of people have been affected by a phobia at some stage in life and that nearly all respondents are acquainted with at least one person who displays phobic symptoms.

Phobia in the past

Phobias appear to be present in all races and cultures although there may be some differences in the prevalence of particular types. They have been mentioned in early historical writings, particularly those of the Greeks and Romans. Allusions are made to phobias in later European writings but by the Middle Ages, they were often regarded as manifestations of demonic activity. Although some phobias have always occurred, for example animal phobias and height phobias, others, particularly those relating to specific diseases or illnesses such as plague, syphilis and rabies, were once more common. These diseases were major killers in the past and, not surprisingly, people were afraid of them.

In the eighteenth and nineteenth centuries, disorders of the mind were once more returned to the realms of medicine and science and attempts were made to study and explain the nature and development of phobias and to treat them. Several misconceptions were born at this time but continuing in-depth study of phobias throughout the twentieth century, particularly during recent years, has shed new light on these fascinating and prevalent disorders and resulted in successful treatment for many phobic sufferers.

Recent developments

The years of research and study by many experts in the field of phobias has led to several new developments. It is generally accepted that:

- there are diagnostic criteria for three clinical categories of phobia.
- the various categories of phobia and individual phobias, themselves, have different causes and reasons (aetiology or aetiological mechanisms) for their development.
- cognitive factors have a part in the development and continuance of phobias. This means that phobias are not entirely unconscious but are, in some cases, and to differing extents, reinforced by a person's perceptions and beliefs about the environment and the phobic stimulus. Recognition of the interplay of different mechanisms and cognitive factors in the development of phobias has challenged earlier, more simplistic theories about their origins.
- increased study and understanding of phobias has led to the development of more helpful specific treatment programmes which can be tailored to individual needs and have proved to be highly successful.

Classification and diagnosis of phobias

(Please note that for the sake of simplicity the phobic person will be assumed to be male in the pages that follow.) Modern psychiatry recognises three major groups of phobia.

1. Agoraphobia
2. Social phobia
3. Specific (single) phobia which includes five subgroups.

The title 'specific' replaces the earlier label of 'simple phobia' which was discarded because it implied that the condition was not serious or distressing.

In the following pages, the first two categories are described in detail along with aspects of their treatment, followed by a general evaluation of the large third group of specific phobias. The subgroups, along with selected examples of specific phobias, are described in more detail on pages 133–213. Chapter 22, the treatments chapter, attempts to define and describe psychotherapeutic approaches and drug treatments with reference to phobias. Alternative therapies, which may be helpful, are described in Chapter 24.

Chapter 2
Agoraphobia

Symptoms and defining criteria

Agoraphobia means, literally, fear (*phobus*) of the marketplace (*agora*). More practically, a sufferer is afraid of being in open, public or crowded places, especially if there is no easy or readily accessible escape route. Many agoraphobics are additionally afraid of becoming mentally and/or physically incapacitated by fear or panic in these circumstances, particularly that they will lose control and be left helpless in front of strangers.

The exact nature of the feared situation varies from one sufferer to another with some agoraphobics being more afraid of open places where there are few people while others can cope better if it is dark or if they are accompanied by a trusted companion. The condition also varies in that, while many agoraphobics experience panic attacks or panic-like symptoms, others do not.

However, in all but the mildest cases, agoraphobia interferes significantly with normal life as the person typically avoids encountering the feared situation. Hence shopping, travelling on public transport, going to the cinema or a football match or indeed to any public venue, including visiting the doctor's surgery, a child's school or the bank, can all become impossible for an agoraphobic. In the most severe cases, avoidance is such that the sufferer becomes totally housebound.

Agoraphobia is a relatively common disorder affecting about four per cent of females and two per cent of males in any half-yearly period. The most likely age at which it makes its first appearance is during the early twenties. Agoraphobia rarely presents itself for the first time after the age of forty.

Many experts recognise the existence of two forms of the disorder: agoraphobia without a history of panic attacks and agoraphobia with panic attacks (or panic disorder). The second form is termed 'panic disorder with agoraphobia' in American psychiatric medicine.

The symptoms and criteria that might be likely to lead to a diagnosis of agoraphobia can be summarised as follows:

- acute anxiety about the thought or reality of being in a (public) place or situation from which there is no easy means of escape. In these circumstances the person may experience feelings of unease that can vary in intensity.
- these places or situations are either avoided or only endured with great difficulty or with the help of a trusted companion.

- both of the above cannot be accounted for by some other mental disorder, physical illness or the effects of drugs or alcohol.

The symptoms and criteria which might lead a clinician to suspect agoraphobia with panic attacks are the same as the above but with the addition of the following

- the experience of one or more panic attacks in the agoraphobic situation and the persistent fear that these might recur.
- anxiety about the possible consequences of the panic attacks such as displaying visible physical symptoms or loss of physical and mental control over one's body.
- changed behaviour as a result of the panic attacks.

Surveys have shown that agoraphobia without panic attacks is much more prevalent than was previously realised and more common than agoraphobia with panic attacks. Some researchers believe that the true picture has been hidden because agoraphobics with panic symptoms are much more likely to seek help and be referred to clinicians. Other 'ordinary' agoraphobics may well remain undiagnosed within the community.

However, since panic attacks or full panic disorder are not infrequently associated with agoraphobia, it becomes helpful to define them at this point.

Panic attacks and disorders

Panic (or anxiety) attack

A panic attack involves the sudden appearance of four or more of the following mental and physical symptoms which are the manifestations of extreme anxiety. These are:

1. Rapid rate of heartbeat or palpitations.
2. Breathlessness or a feeling of being smothered.
3. Tightness or pain in the chest.
4. Tremor, trembling, shaking.
5. Feeling hot or cold or alternating between the two.
6. Shivering or sweating; pallor.
7. Choking feeling in the throat.
8. Dizziness, feelings of faintness or light-headedness.
9. Nausea or gastro-intestinal symptoms.
10. Tingling in the extremities of the limbs or feelings of numbness.
11. Fear that loss of physical control (for example of bladder and bowels) is imminent.
12. Fear that mental collapse and loss of control or 'madness' are imminent.
13. Feelings of detachment and unreality and fear that one may be dying.

The symptoms rapidly reach a peak of intensity within ten minutes of first appearing and then disappear as quickly as they arose. Although a panic attack can be extremely distressing, it is not physically harmful although the sufferer frequently believes that it is. Panic attacks are extremely common with about a third of people experiencing one in any given year.

Panic (or anxiety) disorder

Panic disorder is characterised by the occurrence of panic attacks which, at least in the first instance, arise unexpectedly and are not attached to a particular situation or stimulus. Anticipatory anxiety about the occurrence of further spontaneous attacks is a major part of the disorder. In many, but not all, cases the person avoids the place or situation where a panic attack occurred and this aspect has a strong correlation with agoraphobia.

The person also commonly believes that the panic attack is symptomatic of a serious physical disorder, such as a brain tumour or heart condition, and may report to a doctor or hospital on this basis. A diagnosis of panic disorder is unlikely to be made in these circumstances although it may emerge at a later date. The disorder itself is uncommon, affecting fewer than one in a hundred people in any given six-month period.

Development of agoraphobia

The mechanisms responsible for the development of agoraphobia are extremely complex and remain the subject of a great deal of debate. Numerous theories and models aimed at explaining the nature of the disorder have been put forward by many researchers since the late nineteenth century. Some of these theories are not widely accepted while others have helped to shed light on this complex condition. An understanding of the underlying mechanisms is not only of interest in itself but is of particular importance in devising effective treatment programmes for individual agoraphobics. The following eight factors appear to be relevant in agoraphobia.

1. Cognitive factors, that is beliefs, play a major role in agoraphobia. The fear involved is closely associated with the (mistaken) belief that the person either cannot escape from the situation or can only do so by behaving in a way that would attract attention. This behaviour is perceived to be, at best, embarrassing and, at worst, involving complete mental and physical collapse with awful personal consequences. The fear, and hence the pattern of agoraphobic avoidance, develops either as a result of actual experiences or because of a strong belief that awful events will occur.

2. Panic symptoms are one of the most common factors associated with agoraphobia and a person may develop the condition following a panic attack. However, other conditions may also lead to the development of a form of agoraphobia, such as epilepsy and the fear of having fits in a public place, osteoporosis and the fear of falling and breaking bones if away from home, incontinence and irritable bowel syndrome and

the fear or being 'caught short' without access to a toilet while away from home. The difference lies in the fact that extreme fear is not usually a factor in these circumstances. Also, panic symptoms may occur for the first time after the development of agoraphobia or not at all. Hence, agoraphobia may be more usefully considered as motivated avoidance with panic being one of a range of significant factors involved.

3. There is evidence that at least in some cases, agoraphobics are less assertive and self-sufficient than other people.

4. Agoraphobics may, in some cases, have a history of school phobia in childhood or come from a family background in which relatives have experienced school phobia or agoraphobia.

5. There may be a greater tendency towards depression in some people with agoraphobia.

6. Agoraphobics with panic attacks have a greater fear of dizziness and a greater belief that they will faint or otherwise lose control, compared to those suffering from panic disorder who do not markedly avoid feared situations. These agoraphobics have a low belief in their ability to cope with panic and a high and strong belief in its catastrophic consequences.

7. Many agoraphobics develop coping or safety-seeking strategies to help them to deal with the disorder. Examples include leaning against a wall or hanging on to a supermarket trolley and believing that by doing this, fainting and/or physical collapse is avoided.

8. The fear and panic symptoms (when present),
    avoidance, coping behaviours and beliefs
    (cognitive factors), all interact with each other in
    agoraphobia.

Treatments for agoraphobia

Behaviour therapy

Classic psychotherapeutic treatments for agoraphobia
have employed a form of behaviour therapy called
exposure therapy (*see* page 229). With support, the
agoraphobic person is gradually and increasingly
exposed or encouraged to confront the feared
situation until habituation takes place.

The idea is that the person's anxiety will decrease as
exposure to the situation is shown not to have the
fearful consequences that he expects, allowing
behavioural change to take place. This type of therapy
may also involve flooding in which the person is
intensively exposed to the feared situation. Methods
to control panic attacks, such as using breathing or
relaxation techniques, may be employed as part of
the treatment (*see* Chapter 24).

Cognitive therapy

Cognitive therapists start from a slightly different
standpoint. They take the view that the extreme
anxiety in agoraphobia is a direct result of a sufferer's
distorted perception of threat and danger in the feared

situation, especially that 'giving way' will take place and will be disastrous. The person typically overestimates the threat and underestimates his ability to cope. An interaction then occurs between the beliefs, anxiety or panic symptoms and safety behaviours such as avoidance or 'coping strategies' which help to maintain the agoraphobia.

Hence a cognitive therapist seeks to identify and change the distorted beliefs and safety or coping strategies by discussion and behavioural experiments. For example, an agoraphobic who believes that fainting in a public place will have dreadful consequences might be asked to observe a simulated fainting by a helper. Feelings of dizziness and faintness are a common symptom of phobia but actual fainting is almost entirely confined to blood–injury–injection phobia (*see* Chapter 12). When the person sees that the feared catastrophic consequences do not take place, his distorted beliefs are well on the way to being challenged and abolished.

Cognitive therapy also seeks to challenge the safety-seeking or coping strategies commonly employed by agoraphobics. For example, the person who believes that his legs will give way under him if he does not lean against a wall or hang on to a supermarket trolley is helped to discover that collapse in these circumstances is extremely difficult to achieve. Following a detailed and thorough discussion, the patient and therapist enter the agoraphobic situation with the sole purpose of conducting a 'leg-collapse experiment'. The patient is not allowed to use his 'safety prop' and as soon as he experiences feelings of leg weakness, is asked to try and make his legs give way. When collapse does not occur, further discussion may ensue to see if there is anything else that the patient can do to make his legs fold under him. These may then be tried, with the same result, so that by the end of the experiments, the patient has begun to realise that his legs cannot fold under him and that he has, all along, been misinterpreting physical bodily sensations. Experiments such as these are held to be of great benefit by some therapists.

Differences between behaviour therapy and cognitive therapy

The differences between the two approaches can perhaps be best understood by considering an illustration. Behavioural therapy may be able to help an agoraphobic to get used to the feared situation by repeated exposure.

However, it is also possible to envisage that the agoraphobic could be employing an undisclosed safety or coping strategy on which he is secretly relying. He might, in fact, have his belief in the effectiveness of this reinforced by exposure alone, that is believing that he can confront the agoraphobic situation better because his safety strategy is working so well. Also, if panic control measures have been strongly taught as a part of behavioural therapy, the patient may subsequently be able to enter the agoraphobic situation only because he now believes that he can avoid catastrophe by employing them. It is then likely that he will not have come to realise that panic symptoms are harmless as this belief is not challenged by control alone. His agoraphobia has been controlled rather than changed and panic control has become a safety or coping strategy in its own right.

In cognitive therapy, panic control would perhaps be viewed as one of several useful measures aimed at changing an agoraphobic's belief in the harmfulness of panic symptoms. In practice, cognitive therapy experiments, such as those described above, have to incorporate exposure, which is a key element of behavioural therapy.

There is, in fact, a considerable degree of overlap between the two approaches. The behavioural approach to agoraphobia, based on exposure therapy, has been proved to be effective in most cases and has also been shown to bring about cognitive changes. Many experts believe that the effectiveness of purely cognitive treatments has not been established or is inferior to that of behavioural therapy. The same view also tends to be taken with regard to combined therapies which have been tried. However, both behavioural and cognitive approaches have been proved valuable in the treatment of panic disorder.

The fact that a high percentage of agoraphobics are helped by behavioural exposure therapy is especially encouraging when one considers that it is generally only the most severely affected patients who seek treatment. As mentioned above, it is thought that many agoraphobics (no doubt including those who see themselves as being less seriously affected) remain 'hidden' within the community and never seek professional help. Hence part of the function of a book such as this should be to stress the importance and effectiveness of treatment compared with suffering the distress of agoraphobia.

Drug therapy

Such drugs as antidepressants or benzodiazepines are occasionally prescribed to help alleviate panic symptoms and/or severe depression, if present. These are prescribed only with great caution, generally for short-term relief and, in the case of benzodiazepines, may have to be discontinued before a programme of behaviour therapy can be started. This is because benzodiazepines may interfere with treatment and also cause dependency and withdrawal symptoms. Antidepressants are preferable in that they do not usually cause dependency but they can, on the other hand, produced unwanted side effects which can make them unacceptable to patients. Behavioural exposure therapy, possibly combined with panic control measures, is regarded by most experts as being the treatment of choice.

Chapter 3
Social Phobia

Symptoms and defining criteria

Social phobias form a group of common anxiety disorders that affect both men and women more or less equally. The most common age for social phobia to appear is between fifteen and twenty years. It can be defined as a clinically severe and irrational anxiety provoked by exposure to a range of social and/or 'performance' situations (for example when the person has a role or function to carry out in front of others). The anxiety frequently leads to avoidance of social situations. This can then result in loneliness, isolation and misery, especially since the person is frequently aware of his loss and desires normal social contact.

A key feature of social phobia is the person's fear that he will experience embarrassment and feel humiliated if his behaviour does not meet his own preconceived standard. The social phobic typically fears that he will behave either inadequately or excessively, or in a manner which will attract the adverse criticism and judgement of others. Commonly, he fears that his anxiety will manifest itself in a visible way such as by blushing, trembling, particularly of the hands, having a quavering voice or stammering, not being able to make eye contact, becoming 'tongue-tied', experiencing nausea, vomiting and the urgent need to urinate.

In European psychiatry, the following criteria are used to make a diagnosis of social phobia:

- the mental and physical symptoms must be related to anxiety rather than secondary to some other condition such as obsessive compulsive disorder or post-traumatic stress disorder
- the anxiety must arise in social situations
- phobic avoidance should be a significant feature.

Specific and general social phobia

Two subgroups of social phobia are recognised – specific and general. In specific social phobia, the anxiety is centred on a particular situation such as making a speech, singing or playing a solo in music, attending an interview, dining out in a social setting, or even writing or signing one's name in front of others or using a public washroom. General social phobia encompasses a much broader range of situations but in both subgroups, the person is normally at ease when performing the same activities at home or within a close circle of family and friends.

Avoidant personality disorder

A further, and the most severe, form of social phobia

is categorised as avoidant personality disorder. These people experience the greatest measurable degrees of distress and avoidance of social situations and are regarded by clinicians as being the most severe cases.

There appears to be a higher incidence of avoidant personality disorder in men than in women and general social phobia is more severe than specific social phobia. Quite commonly, the affected person believes that the physical symptoms of anxiety are the major problem rather than the phobia itself.

Development of social phobia

It is likely that all but the most confident people have experienced a degree of social anxiety or 'nerves' at one stage or another, if only on some 'big' occasion when they have been in the limelight. Many readers will have had experience of the shaking paper notes and nervous voice of the brave person delivering a talk who is unaccustomed to public speaking.

However, many would be able to cope with such an occasion, even if not particularly enjoying it, and would be able to believe that they had the sympathy and interest of their audience. At a party, a person may feel uneasy, or be inclined to compare himself unfavourably with other guests whom he regards as being more attractive or charming than himself. However, such negative feelings would not normally prevent him from going to the party or from enjoying himself once there. The difference in social phobia is that it occurs at the extreme end of a scale which extends beyond reasonable social anxiety. A social phobic would either avoid such situations as those described above or could only endure them with great difficulty and with the accompaniment of highly unpleasant, distressing feelings and symptoms.

Social phobics commonly have low self-esteem, assuming that they are evaluated negatively and critically by others in a social context and fearing such judgements. They may have a critical standard of behaviour which they have set for themselves and, in the phobic situation, they engage in constant self-monitoring for signs that they are falling below the ideal. If the social phobic fails in his own estimation to meet his critical standard, it may have the effect of further undermining his already low self-esteem.

Social phobics may also be on the lookout for signs of negative judgements being made about them by other people. In fact, they may be hypersensitive to perfectly innocuous signs or remarks from others and misinterpret these as criticism. The social phobic is already anxious when he enters the feared situation and may well be in a state of heightened physiological arousal (for example raised heartbeat rate, sweating, etc). It is thought that these physical symptoms reinforce the process of self-monitoring, in that the person believes that they are a sign of impending social failure and that they are highly visible and obvious to others. The person becomes even more self-vigilant which may well have the effect of increasing his physical symptoms of anxiety. All this, combined with his lack of self-worth and low expectations, leads to a reduced likelihood of achieving social success.

Other people may indeed notice the anxiety of the social phobic. However, a number of experimental studies have shown that an impartial observer invariably rates the social phobic's performance much more highly than the sufferer does himself. Other experiments have proved that the social phobic almost always attaches a self-critical evaluation to circumstances which are neutral or ambiguous. For example, if friends at a home dinner party excuse themselves and leave early, the social phobic is much more likely to believe that it is due to their dissatisfaction with him rather than any other explanation. Also, even if the social phobic receives clearly encouraging or positive feedback from other people, he usually attributes it to external factors unconnected with himself such as the overall happy atmosphere at a party.

Although internal self-focused behaviour in accordance with that described above is a factor in most emotional disorders, including some other phobias, it has been proposed that it is particularly critical in social phobia.

Other cognitive factors are also considered by several experts to be important in maintaining social phobia.

These are the phobic's anticipatory anxiety about an impending social event, his 'post-mortem' analysis of it, his possible deployment of safety behaviours within it or his complete avoidance of the situation. Anticipation of the event fuels the start of anxiety and negative self-focused thoughts that is reported by many social phobics. It includes mentally reviewing what is likely to happen in a negative way and working on any safety behaviours that might be employed. Current thoughts may be influenced by memories of events from the past which were deemed to be awful. Anticipation may lead to complete avoidance but, if not, it has the effect of ensuring that the person enters the situation in heightened anxiety or self-monitoring mode.

The social phobic's troubles are not necessarily over once he has endured the event. In many cases, the person minutely reviews every aspect of the event, concentrating on himself and his performance and invariably evaluating it in a negative way, which causes more distress and feeds the phobia for the future.

As in agoraphobia, the deployment of safety behaviours to avert the feared, supposedly catastrophic consequences of failure, are a common feature of social phobia.

Safety behaviours

Safety behaviours take different forms but are often concentrated on measures to disguise the manifestations of anxiety. Examples include holding oneself rigid or using a support such as a wall to hide trembling, not drinking, except when no one is looking, to prevent shaking hands (and the possibility of spillage) from being noticed, and wearing several layers of light-coloured clothes to conceal sweating. Also, the person may mentally rehearse what he will say, concentrating on pronunciation and getting sentences exactly right, perhaps trying to stick to a preconceived pattern of conversation.

In reality, safety behaviours generally serve to exacerbate the symptoms that the social phobic is at such pains to conceal. Holding oneself rigid makes movement less co-ordinated and more noticeably odd. Wearing lots of clothes increases sweating and rehearsed conversation is more likely to sound strange, stilted and aloof. Hence, the feared outcome of behaving in a way that is noticeable to others and that may attract adverse reaction, is rendered more likely in these circumstances. Also, the deployment of safety behaviours has the effect of increasing and maintaining the person's self-focused attention. He is less likely to detect favourable social cues from others because he is concentrating so hard on maintaining his 'safety shield' and so is not attuned to those around him.

Finally, as has been suggested in agoraphobia, the social phobic may come to believe that it is the successful deployment of safety behaviour that saves him from disaster. He may believe that he has 'survived' in the phobic setting only because the safety strategy has worked and saved him from notice, embarrassment or humiliation. If this is the case, then safety behaviours are clearly detrimental and serve only to ensure the continuance of the phobia. Avoidance is, of course, the most extreme form of 'safety behaviour'. The person avoids all the anticipatory, actual and post-mortem anxiety of social events but, in so doing, inevitably maintains the fear and the phobia. As in other types of phobia, avoidance ensures that disconfirmation of fear and catastrophe can never take place.

Treatments for social phobia

Behaviour therapy and cognitive therapy

In the past, classical treatments for social phobia encompassed psychotherapy and medication. More specifically, the type of psychotherapy used was the form of behaviour therapy called exposure therapy in which the social phobic is exposed in various ways to the phobic situation. This was often combined with social skills training on the assumption that part of the problem was that the phobic person was deficient in this area. Exposure and social skills training proved effective in helping some (but not all) sufferers but was superior to no treatment at all.

However, in modern treatment practice, there is far less emphasis on social skills training, although it may still be included as part of a therapy programme. This is due to the fact that a lack of social skills is not now generally regarded as being the primary problem in social phobia. Exposure therapy remains an important treatment tool although some therapists believe that its effectiveness is limited because they hold that it does not, in itself, bring about belief (cognitive) change.

In recent years, various forms of cognitive therapy have been used in the treatment of social phobia which have usually involved aspects of rational emotive therapy and self-instructional training. Other therapists have employed combined behavioural-cognitive treatments, perhaps involving exposure, anxiety control and challenges to the mistaken beliefs and assumptions at work in social phobia. Different therapists may recommend particular types or combinations of treatment and some may match individual patients to the form that they feel will be most beneficial to them.

A considerable number of studies have been carried out in an attempt to determine whether one particular type or combination of therapy is more effective in treating social phobia. Different researchers have had differing results so that the picture remains unclear with further studies continuing to be carried out.

At present, no form of therapy has been proved to be unequivocally more effective than another but all are better than no treatment at all.

Drug therapy

Various drugs have been used in the treatment of social phobia and have proved to be helpful in some cases. They include monoamine oxidase inhibitors, especially phenelzine (sulphate), which act against depression and anxiety and selective serotonin re-uptake inhibitors such as sertraline. Also, the newer benzodiazepines such as clonazepan have been shown to help some sufferers. The tranquilliser and anxiolytic drug, buspirone (hydrochloride) and fluoextine have also been used. One final drug group that has been tried are the Beta blockers. These act on the sympathetic nervous system and are primarily used in the treatment of high blood pressure, but they also appear to have anti-anxiety effects in some cases.

Clinicians have reported favourable results in some, but by no means all, patients with social phobia. In general, it appears that some patients can be helped by drug treatment, at least in the short term, but there is uncertainty with regard to longer-term benefits. Some therapists have combined drug treatments with psychotherapy (exposure) but with mixed results. There is controversy as to whether the use of drugs interferes with or enhances psychotherapy with the latter remaining the treatment of choice.

Chapter 4
Specific Phobia

Symptoms and defining criteria

Specific phobia can be broadly described as an extreme and inappropriate fear provoked by a particular, single object or situation. The range of stimuli that can provoke a specific phobic response is extremely broad and varied. The fear produced is of clinical significance and is frequently sufficiently distressing to result in complete avoidance of the stimulus. The degree of disruption of normal life and activity depends upon the nature of the stimulus and the ease with which it can be avoided. Some situations and objects are obviously less frequently encountered than others and hence cause fewer problems. Nonetheless, the distress and worry caused by a specific phobia are very real and can be extremely disruptive of normal life.

The American Psychiatric Association has produced a list of criteria that are used to define specific phobia and that can be briefly summarised as follows:

- an extreme and excessive fear that is provoked by a particular object (either animate or inanimate) or situation. The fearful state may also be elicited by thoughts or anticipation of the stimulus and is present for a prolonged period of time should the specific circumstances arise.

- the fear occurs immediately in response to the exposure to the phobic stimulus and may take the form of a panic attack.
- the person is aware that his fear is excessive or out of proportion although this may not be so if the sufferer is a young child.
- the phobic stimulus can only be endured with extreme anxiety or distress or else is avoided altogether.
- the existence of the phobia causes the person embarrassment or distress or it has a significant effect upon normal life activities.
- in a child under eighteen years of age, the phobia must persist for at least six months. Also, it is recognised that a child will express his fear in childish ways such as crying and screaming, clinging, refusal to stay in bed, etc.
- the fear and phobic avoidance cannot be attributed to agoraphobia, social phobia or any other anxiety disorder such as obsessive-compulsive disorder, post-traumatic stress disorder or separation anxiety disorder including school phobia (*see* Chapter 5).

The existence of what might be termed 'normal childhood fears' is recognised in this list of criteria. As any parent knows, fears and anxieties quite commonly arise in children and can be intense and distressing. Usually, however, these subside as a child

35

grows in age and understanding or do not cause the intense distress that accompanies a phobia.

In addition to the criteria listed above, the American Psychiatric Association has identified five subgroups of specific phobia as follows:

1. Animal phobias – provoked by exposure to particular species such as spiders, snakes, cats, dogs or sometimes several species, e.g. flying insects.
2. Natural environment phobia – provoked by exposure to, for example, storms, water (rivers, sea, waterfalls), high places, woods and forests.
3. Blood–injury–injection phobia – provoked by the sight of blood, accidental injuries, anything connected with surgical needles (giving blood or blood sample, receiving vaccination) or other surgical procedures.
4. Situational phobia – provoked by exposure to, for example, enclosed spaces (*see* claustrophobia, Chapter 13)) such as lifts or tunnels, flying in aeroplanes or using other forms of transport, crossing a bridge. Although there is some degree of overlap, the 'situations' are more likely to be man-made as opposed to those in the natural environment.
5. Other phobias – provoked by a broad range of stimuli which cannot easily be assigned to the other subgroups. Examples include: phobias relating to exposure to particular diseases, illnesses or conditions, such as AIDS, choking (*see*

Chapter 18) and vomiting; objects such as glass, mirrors, statues; or particular types of people, for example clowns or those in costume. If a person wrongly believes, against all evidence, that he has contracted a particular disease or condition, it is regarded as being a hypochondriacal or delusional disorder in European psychiatry.

Specific phobias are the most prevalent of the three categories and also the most common of the anxiety disorders, affecting about seven per cent of women and about four per cent of men during any half-yearly period that is selected at random. Overall, specific phobias affect about five per cent of children, may be present with other anxiety disorders, such as separation anxiety, and may be slightly more common in girls than in boys.

However, the true figure is likely to be even higher since it is known that many sufferers are able to avoid encounters with their phobic stimulus, do not seek treatment and may not admit to the existence of their phobia. In fact, avoidance is the most common 'safety-seeking' behaviour for those with a specific phobia. (Compare agoraphobia [Chapter 2] and social phobia [Chapter 3]).

Development of specific phobia

Many detailed studies into the nature and development of specific phobias have been carried out and these have contributed a great deal towards current understanding of phobias as a whole. This research, conducted over many years, has produced a number of theories concerning the mechanisms underlying the acquisition and maintenance of specific phobias. In many cases, there may be several factors at work and these may interact with one another (*see* Chapter 21). Although there is no universal acceptance among experts of any particular theory, the research has not only been of interest in itself but has also led to the development of particular treatment programmes for some specific phobias.

Treatments for specific phobia

In general, some form of exposure (behaviour) therapy remains the treatment of choice for most types of specific phobia. Some therapists have achieved encouraging results using cognitive approaches, combined behavioural and cognitive treatments and matched treatments but the results are not clear cut. Drug treatments are generally not regarded as being helpful in the treatment of specific phobia. Most sufferers can be helped by modern therapy programmes and many can learn to cope with their phobia so that it is no longer a problem for them in everyday life.

Due to the intense nature of phobic fear, sufferers may feel reluctant to seek help, believing that the cure may be worse than the condition. Hence it is important to stress that in modern therapy, nothing happens without full discussion and explanation and the consent and co-operation of the patient at every stage. In contrast with the sudden and unexpected encounters with the phobic stimulus that may take place in real life, therapy provides a controlled and gradual exposure. Once one goal has been achieved, with the aid and support of the therapist, the patient is encouraged to move on to a second and further stages which usually involve greater exposure or closer encounters with the feared stimulus.

Chapter 5
Anxiety Disorders

Specific phobias, at least in children, can co-exist with some other anxiety disorders. Also, in order for a diagnosis of phobia to be made, a clinician must first eliminate these other anxiety disorders. Hence it is helpful at this point to include a brief description of these in order to compare and contrast them with phobias.

Obsessive-compulsive disorder

Obsessive-compulsive disorder is an anxiety disorder in which the person is greatly troubled by intrusive and unwelcome thoughts, images, imagined events, urges or ideas. These thoughts arise spontaneously, or at least are not consciously summoned by the person, and cause a variety of unwelcome emotions ranging from anxiety to disgust. The person finds the intrusive thoughts bizarre, embarrassing, morbid or repugnant and, characteristically, carries out repeated ritualised behaviours in order to counteract them.

Examples of ritualised behaviour include continual hand washing (to counteract fears about dirt or contamination), repeated checking to see if switches or controls are turned off or doors are locked, performing a bizarre routine before doing something and repeating words or phrases or counting. Often, the ritualised behaviour cannot logically relieve the obsession but performing it provides the person with some relief and comfort. Sufferers are usually aware, even if only to a small extent, that their obsession and ritualised behaviour is excessive but they cannot help themselves.

Since they are aware that their behaviour is likely to appear odd to others, they may well go to great lengths to conceal its existence. This leads to a great deal of stress and it is estimated that one third of obsessive-compulsive disorder patients also suffer from depression. The disorder affects equal numbers of men and women and about 1.6 per cent of people are affected at any one time during a randomly selected, half-yearly period.

Post-traumatic stress disorder

Post-traumatic stress disorder is caused, in the first instance, by experiencing and surviving a severely traumatic event or series of events. The experience evoked terror and feelings of helplessness, despair and pain. Often, the person's own life was in danger or he may have suffered severe injury and frequently, the event involved the death, injury and suffering of those around him. Afterwards, when the person has returned to a safe environment or has recovered physically, the experience comes back to 'haunt' him as a series of flashbacks and/or nightmares. The original, frightening and painful emotions are experienced over again and the person often additionally suffers from depression and feelings of guilt, especially if he has survived when others did not (survivor guilt).

The sufferer typically avoids places or situations which may trigger memories or flashbacks such as watching films about a similar disaster. He may undergo personality changes, particularly becoming withdrawn and less emotionally responsive, both to the outside world and those closest to him. Other physical symptoms include sleep disturbance, irritability, heightened anxiety, loss of memory, inability to concentrate or to perform everyday tasks or one's job, headaches and vertigo. Some degree of re-experience of traumatic events is considered usual (*see* acute stress disorder, below). However, if it is persistent, that is continues for more than three months (or, in many cases, for years), a diagnosis of chronic post-traumatic stress disorder is likely to be made.

Acute stress disorder

Acute stress disorder is similar to post-traumatic stress disorder in its symptoms but differs in duration. It arises promptly, within one month of the traumatic event, and persists for between two and four weeks. The person typically experiences feelings of detachment and unreality, inability to concentrate or reduced awareness of things around him and numbing of emotions. There may be loss of memory of some parts of the trauma. In general, this may be considered to be a natural response to a dreadful event. Given appropriate and sympathetic support, particularly the opportunity to talk about the trauma and the way they are feeling, many people recover and are able to move on from the experience.

Generalised anxiety disorder

This disorder is characterised by the occurrence of excessive and inappropriate levels of anxiety concerning a number of aspects of everyday life. The anxiety is so severe that the person finds it difficult to cope and to function effectively and he is worried most of the time. The level of anxiety may fluctuate but it is generally present in the background and comes to the fore if the person feels under stress.

Matters concerning work, family, finance, health, personal safety and that of those close to the sufferer and household responsibilities are all common areas of anxiety. Also, the anxiety experienced is general rather than being centred on one particular situation or set of circumstances and the person is not usually concerned about the responses or reactions of others.

Symptoms include sleep disturbance, tiredness, inability to concentrate, irritability, muscle tension, headaches and restlessness. The disorder tends to be persistent and chronic and is prevalent, affecting between three per cent and five per cent of the population at any particular period but being twice as common in women than in men. It is usually treated with drugs such as benzodiazepines, other anxiolytics or antidepressants but these relieve symptoms rather than providing a cure. Severely affected patients may be referred for psychotherapy and several alternative therapies and self-help measures may also prove beneficial to individual sufferers (*see* Chapter 24).

Anxiety due to a physical disorder or substance

As indicated by the title, anxiety may arise as a result of the occurrence of many different physical diseases. Additionally it can be caused by the use or abuse of prescription or over-the-counter drugs, alcohol, caffeine and illegal substances. Anxiety is a common withdrawal symptom experienced by persons trying to come off addictive or other potent substances. Treatment is aimed at the cause of the anxiety in the first instance, whether this is a physical disease or substance-induced. Once this has been completed, further treatment for persistent anxiety may be needed in the form of psychotherapy, appropriate drug therapy or, possibly, alternative therapies.

Separation anxiety

A state of extreme anxiety and distress affecting children caused by actual or anticipated separation from their parents and their secure, home surroundings. It commonly occurs in a baby who is parted from his mother or who reacts to being approached or picked up by a stranger. However, it can also occur in older children, most commonly when they have to start school.

It can be seen that each of these anxiety disorders have characteristics which distinguish them from phobias although in individual cases, the situation may not always be initially clear. Hence the first task of a clinician is to arrive at an appropriate diagnosis by thorough examination and discussion of symptoms with the patient.

Chapter 6
A List of Phobias

Phobia (Phobia stimulus, i.e. extreme fear of)	Classification (Medical classification, if applicable)	American Name/s (American names that have been applied)
Abandonment – being abandoned or forgotten	Specific phobia Others subgroup	Athagoraphobia
Accidents – usually as a result of a previous road accident	Specific phobia Situational subgroup Accident phobia	Dystychiphobia
AIDS	Specific phobia Others subgroup Disease phobia	Molysomophobia
Air pollution – being contaminated by, or ingesting, airborne toxins or germs	Specific phobia Others subgroup	Misophobia Molysomophobia Aerophobia

47

Phobia	Classification	American Name/s
Air sickness – vomiting specifically caused by flying	Specific phobia Others subgroup	Aeronausiphobia
Alcohol – alcoholic drinks	Specific phobia Others subgroup	Methyphobia Potophobia
Amnesia – fear of extreme memory loss and loss of identity	Specific phobia Others subgroup	Amnesiphobia
Amphibians – either all kinds (frogs, toads, newts) or limited to combinations of species	Specific phobia Animals subgroup	Batrachophobia
Amputees – fear of people with amputations	Specific phobia Others subgroup	Apotemnophobia

Phobia	Classification	American Name/s
Anger – fear of anger in oneself or others	Specific phobia Others subgroup	Angrophobia Choleraphobia
Angina – fear of severe chest pain and heart attack	Specific phobia Others subgroup	Anginophobia
Animals – generalised fear of animals	Specific phobia Animals subgroup	Zoophobia
Ants	Specific phobia Animals subgroup	Myrmecophobia
Asymmetry and asymmetrical objects and shapes	Specific phobia Others subgroup	Asymmetriphobia

49

Phobia	Classification	American Name/s
Ataxia – fear of the shaky movements and loss of coordination accompanying certain central nervous system disorders. Fear of affected people or being affected oneself.	Specific phobia Others subgroup Disease phobia	Ataxiphobia
Atomic accidents and explosions – both bombs and nuclear plant disasters	Specific phobia Others subgroup	Atomosophobia
Bacteria, microbes and viruses – fear of disease-causing pathogens	Specific phobia Others subgroup	Bacteriophobia Verminophobia Microphobia Sperm or Spermatophobia

Phobia	Classification	American Name/s
Baldness – fear of baldness in others or becoming bald	Specific phobia Others subgroup	Peladophobia, Phalacrophobia
Bathing and washing	Specific phobia Others subgroup Water phobia	Ablutophobia
Bats – fear that bats may land on or attack the person or get caught in hair	Specific phobia Animals subgroup	Chiropterophobia
Beards and bearded men	Specific phobia Others subgroup	Pogonophobia
Being seen – fear of being seen or stared at	Specific phobia Others subgroup	Ophthalmophobia Scopophobia

Phobia	Classification	American Name/s
Beautiful women	Specific phobia Others subgroup	Caligyne phobia Venustraphobia
Bed – fear of going to bed	Specific phobia Situational phobia	Clinophobia
Bees – fear of bees and of being stung	Specific phobia Animals subgroup	Apiphobia Melissophobia
Beggars and tramps – fear of dishevelled or 'out-of-the-ordinary' people	Specific phobia Others subgroup	Hobophobia
Bicycles	Specific phobia Others subgroup	Cyclophobia

Phobia	Classification	American Name/s
Birds – sometimes especially birds in flight; may be restricted to certain species or generalised fear	Specific phobia Animals subgroup	Ornithophobia
Black – the colour black, blackness	Specific phobia Others subgroup Colour phobia	Melanophobia
Blindness – blind people or becoming blind oneself	Specific phobia Others subgroup	Scotomaphobia
Blood – sight of blood, donating blood, bleeding as a result of accidental injury; often also injections	Specific phobia Blood–injury–injection subgroup	Hemophobia Hemaphobia Hematophobia

Phobia	Classification	American Name/s
Blushing – fear of blushing in front of others	Specific phobia Others subgroup	Ereuthrophobia
Body odours – fear of detecting these in others (or oneself)	Specific phobia Others subgroup	Autodysomophobia Bromidrosiphobia Bromidrophobia
'Bogeymen' – fear of non-existent, imagined threatening figures	Specific phobia Others subgroup	Bogeyphobia
Books	Specific phobia Others subgroup	Bibliophobia
Bound – being bound, tied up	Specific phobia Others subgroup or Situational subgroup Claustrophobia	Merinthophobia

Phobia	Classification	American Name/s
Brain disease – fear of affliction with (incurable or progressive) brain disease or condition, in oneself or in others	Specific phobia Others subgroup	Meningitophobia
Bridges (and tunnels)	Specific phobia Situational subgroup	Gephyrophobia Claustrophobia
Bullets and missiles	Specific phobia Others subgroup	Ballistophobia
Bulls	Specific phobia Animals subgroup	Taurophobia
Buried alive	Specific phobia Situational subgroup	Taphephobia Taphophobia

Phobia	Classification	American Name/s
Butterflies, moths, flying insects – fear of the fluttering flight of these insects and that they might alight on the person	Specific phobia Animals subgroup	Mottephobia
Buttons	Specific phobia Others subgroup	Vestiphobia
Cancer – fear of getting cancer oneself or of the disease in others	Specific phobia Others subgroup Disease phobia	Cancerophobia Carcinophobia
Car journeys or cars	Specific phobia Situational subgroup	Amaxophobia Motor phobia

Phobia	Classification	American Name/s
Cats	Specific phobia Animals subgroup	Ailurophobia Elurophobia Felinophobia Galeophobia Gatophobia
Causing embarrassment to others	Taijin-Kyofu-Sho Specific phobia Others subgroup	Taijin-Kyofu-Sho
Celestial bodies – stars, planets, sun, moon, comets, meteors, cosmic events	Specific phobia Natural environment subgroup	Cometophobia
Cemeteries	Specific phobia Situational subgroup	Coimetophobia Kosmikophobia

Understanding Phobias

Phobia	Classification	American Name/s
Ceremonies and ceremonial occasions	Specific phobia Others subgroup	Teleophobia
Changes and new developments in life	Specific phobia Others subgroup	Metathesiophobia
Chemicals	Specific phobia Others subgroup	Chemophobia
Chickens and poultry	Specific phobia Animals subgroup	Alektorophobia
Childbirth – usually fear of (pregnancy and) childbirth	Specific phobia Others subgroup	Lockiophobia Maieusiophobia Parturiphobia

Phobia	Classification	American Name/s
Children	Specific phobia Others subgroup	Pedophobia
Chinese – fear of Chinese people and Chinese culture	Specific phobia Others subgroup	Sinophobia
Chins	Specific phobia Others subgroup	Geniophobia
Chocolate	Specific phobia Others subgroup	Xocolatophobia
Choking – fear of choking on food, pills, etc	Specific phobia Others subgroup Choking phobia	Anginophobia

59

Phobia	Classification	American Name/s
Cholera	Specific phobia Others subgroup Disease phobia	Cholerophobia
Churches	Specific phobia Situational subgroup	Ecclesiophobia
Clocks	Specific phobia Others subgroup	Chronomentrophobia
Clothing	Specific phobia Others subgroup	Vestiphobia
Clouds	Specific phobia Natural environment subgroup	Neophophobia

Phobia	Classification	American Name/s
Clowns	Specific phobia Others subgroup	Coulrophobia
Coitus – fear of sexual act	Specific phobia Others subgroup	Coitophobia
Cold – extreme cold (snow, ice, frost)	Specific phobia Natural environment subgroup	Cheimaphobia Cheimatophobia Cryophobia Frigophobia Psychrophobia
Colours	Specific phobia Others subgroup	Chromophobia Chromatophobia

Phobia	Classification	American Name/s
Computers	Specific phobia Others subgroup	Cyberphobia Logizomechano-phobia
Confined spaces – fear of small, enclosed spaces	Specific phobia Situational subgroup Claustrophobia	Claustrophobia
Constipation – fear of developing this condition and of discomfort and pain in defecation	Specific phobia Others subgroup	Coprastasophobia Defecaloesiophobia
Contagion and contamination – being contaminated with germs or dirt; fear of being contagious oneself or in contact with contagious people	Specific phobia Others subgroup	Tapinophobia

Phobia	Classification	American Name/s
Cooking	Specific phobia Others subgroup	Mageirocophobia
Crawling creatures – fear of (usually) crawling insects	Specific phobia Animals subgroup	Entomophbia
Crosses and crucifixes, crossroads	Specific phobia Others subgroup	Staurophobia
Crossing bridges – sometimes part of height phobia	Specific phobia Situational subgroup	Gephyrophobia Gephydrophobia Gephysrophobia
Crossing roads	Specific phobia Situational subgroup	Agyrophobia Dromophobia

Phobia	Classification	American Name/s
Crowds and crowded places	Agoraphobia	Demophobia Enochlophobia Ochlophobia
Crystalline substances and crystals	Specific phobia Others subgroup	Crystallophobia
Dancing	Specific phobia Others subgroup	Chorophobia
Darkness and night-time	Specific phobia Natural environment subgroup	Achulophobia Chorophobia Lygophobia Myctophobia Nyctophobia

Phobia	Classification	American Name/s
Dawn and daytime, daylight	Specific phobia Natural environment subgroup	Eosophobia Phengophobia
Death, dead bodies	Specific phobia Others subgroup	Necrophobia Thanatophobia Thantophobia
Decay and decaying matter	Specific phobia Natural environment subgroup	Seplophobia
Decision-making	Specific phobia Others subgroup	Decidophobia
Defecation	Specific phobia Others subgroup	Rhypophobia

Phobia	Classification	American Name/s
Defeat – fear of being defeated in life situations	Specific phobia Others subgroup	Kakorrhaphio-phobia
Deformity – in others or becoming so oneself	Specific phobia Others subgroup	Dysmorphophobia Teratophobia
Dentists and dental treatment	Specific phobia Others subgroup	Dentophobia
Dependence – becoming dependent on others and helpless	Specific phobia Others subgroup	Soteriophobia
Depth and deep, cavernous places	Specific phobia Natural environment subgroup	Bathophobia

Phobia	Classification	American Name/s
Devil, devils and demons	Specific phobia Others subgroup	Demonoorphobia Daemonophobia Satan phobia
Diabetes – becoming diabetic or diabetes in others	Specific phobia Others subgroup Disease phobia	Diabetophobia
Dining out, dinner parties – social dining	Social phobia	Deipnophobia
Dirt, dust or becoming dirty oneself	Specific phobia Others subgroup	Amathophobia Automysophobia Koniophobia Mysophobia Rupophobia

Phobia	Classification	American Name/s
Disease – diseases in general or specific ones	Specific phobia Others subgroup Disease phobia	Monopathophobia Panthopathophobia Pathophobia
Disorder and untidiness	Specific phobia Others subgroup	Ataxophobia
Dizziness	Specific phobia Others subgroup	Dinophobia
Doctors	Specific phobia Others subgroup	Iatrophobia
Dogs	Specific phobia Animals subgroup Dog phobia	Cynophobia

Phobia	Classification	American Name/s
Dolls	Specific phobia Others subgroup Doll phobia	Pediophobia
Double vision	Specific phobia Others subgroup	Diplophobia
Dreams	Specific phobia Others subgroup	Oneirophobia
Drinking	Specific phobia Others subgroup	Dipsophobia
Drugs and medicines	Specific phobia Others subgroup	Pharmacophobia

Phobia	Classification	American Name/s
Dryness	Specific phobia Others subgroup	Xerophobia
Dutch people and culture	Specific phobia Others subgroup	Dutchphobia
Electricity	Specific phobia Others subgroup	Electrophobia
English people and English culture	Specific phobia Others subgroup	Anglophobia
Epilepsy – fear of developing the condition and of encountering it in others	Specific phobia Others subgroup Disease phobia	Hyelephobia (also used for materialism)

Phobia	Classification	American Name/s
Erection – fear of losing erection	Specific phobia Others subgroup	Medomalacuphobia
Eye patches – fear of people with eye patches and of the patches themselves	Specific phobia Others subgroup	
Eyes	Specific phobia Others subgroup	Ommetaphobia Ommetophobia
Fabrics – fear of particular textiles, e.g. wool	Specific phobia Others subgroup	Textophobia
Faeces	Specific phobia Others subgroup	Coprophobia Scatophobia

Phobia	Classification	American Name/s
Failure – fear of the opinions of others or the consequences of failure	Specific phobia Others subgroup	Atychiphobia Kakorrhaphiophobia
Fainting (often as a part of blood–injury–injection phobia)	Specific phobia Others subgroup	Asthenophobia
Falling (often as a part of height phobia)	Specific phobia Others subgroup	Basiphobia Basophobia
Falsehood – being lied to by others or lying oneself	Specific phobia Others subgroup	Mythophobia
Fatigue	Specific phobia Others subgroup	Kopophobia
Feathers – fear of being touched by feathers	Specific phobia Others subgroup	Pteronophobia

Phobia	Classification	American Name/s
Fever – becoming feverish or seeing fever in others	Specific phobia Others subgroup	Febriphobia Fibriophobia Fibriphobia Pyrexiophobia
Fire	Specific phobia Others subgroup	Arsonphobia Pyrophobia
Firearms	Specific phobia Others subgroup	Hoplophobia
Fish	Specific phobia Animals subgroup	Icthyophobia
Flashing lights	Specific phobia Others subgroup	Selaphobia

Phobia	Classification	American Name/s
Flowers	Specific phobia Others subgroup	Anthophobia Anthrophobia
Flutes	Specific phobia Others subgroup	Aulophobia
Flying	Specific phobia Situational subgroup Flight phobia	Aviaphobia Aviophobia Pteromerhano- phobia
Flying creatures – generalised fear of flying animals	Animal phobia	Ornithophobia
Fog	Specific phobia Natural environment subgroup	Homichlophobia Nebulaphobia

Phobia	Classification	American Name/s
Food and/or eating	Specific phobia Others subgroup	Antlophobia Sitiophobia Sitophobia
Food – sometimes specific foods or related to choking phobia	Specific phobia Others subgroup	Cibophobia Sitiophobia Sitophobia
Foreigners	Specific phobia Others subgroup	Xenophobia
Forests and woodlands	Specific phobia Natural environment subgroup	Hylophobia
Forgotten or forgetting	Specific phobia Others subgroup	Athazagora-phobia

Phobia	Classification	American Name/s
French people or culture	Specific phobia Others subgroup	Francophobia Galiophobia Gallophobia
Friday 13th	Specific phobia Others subgroup	Paraskavedekatria-phobia
Frogs	Specific phobia Animals subgroup	Ranidaphobia
Furs and skins of animals	Specific phobia Others subgroup	Doraphobia
Gaiety	Specific phobia Others subgroup	Cherophobia

Phobia	Classification	American Name/s
Garlic	Specific phobia Others subgroup	Alliumphobia
Genitals – both or either male or female	Specific phobia Others subgroup	Kolpophobia Eurotophobia (female)
German people and culture, Germany	Specific phobia Others subgroup	Germanophobia Teutophobia
Ghosts, spirits, spectres – fear of encountering a supernatural being, or anything relating to the supernatural	Specific phobia Others subgroup	Phasmophobia Pneumatiphobia Spectrophobia
Glaring, dazzling lights such as searchlights	Specific phobia Others subgroup	Photoaugliaphobia

77

Phobia	Classification	American Name/s
Glass	Specific phobia Others subgroup	Hyalophobia Hyelophobia Nelophobia
God, gods and religious rituals and ceremonies	Specific phobia Others subgroup	Theophobia Zeusophobia
Gold	Specific phobia Others subgroup	Aurophobia
Going out alone (can be a part of agoraphobia)	Specific phobia Others subgroup	Isolophobia Autophobia
Good news	Specific phobia Others subgroup	Euphobia

Phobia	Classification	American Name/s
Gravity	Specific phobia Others subgroup	Barophobia
Great mole rat	Specific phobia Animals subgroup	Zemmiphobia
Greek words and scientific terms	Specific phobia Others subgroup	Hellenologophobia
Hair	Specific phobia Others subgroup	Chaetophobia Hypertrichophobia Trichopathophobia Trichophobia
Hallowe'en	Specific phobia Others subgroup	Samhainophobia

Phobia	Classification	American Name/s
Handwriting – handwritten script	Specific phobia Others subgroup	Graphophobia
Heat	Specific phobia Others subgroup	Thermophobia
Heart – fear of one's heart ceasing to beat or heart attack or of the organ itself	Specific phobia Others subgroup	Cardiophobia
Heaven	Specific phobia Others subgroup	Ouranophobia Uranophobia
Heights – fear of all high places and ladders	Specific phobia Others subgroup Height phobia (Acrophobia)	Acrophobia Altophobia Batophobia Hypsiphobia

Phobia	Classification	American Name/s
Hell	Specific phobia Others subgroup	Hadephobia Stigiophobia Stygiophobia
Heredity and hereditary conditions	Specific phobia Others subgroup	Patroiophobia
Heresy – challenges to authority and official doctrine	Specific phobia Others subgroup	Hereiophobia Heresyphobia
Home and home surroundings, going home	Specific phobia Situational subgroup	Ecophobia Eicophobia Nostophobia Oikophobia
Homosexuals and homosexuality	Specific phobia Others subgroup	Homophobia

Phobia	Classification	American Name/s
Horses	Specific phobia Animals subgroup	Equinophobia Hippophobia
Hospitals	Specific phobia Situational subgroup	Nosocomephobia
Houses	Specific phobia Others subgroup	Domatophobia Oikophobia
Hurricanes and tornadoes	Specific phobia Natural environment subgroup	Lilapsophobia
Hypnosis	Specific phobia Others subgroup	Hypnophobia

Phobia	Classification	American Name/s
Ice and frost, *see also* cold	Specific phobia Natural environment subgroup	Pagophobia
Ideas	Specific phobia Others subgroup	Toleophobia
Illness, *see also* disease	Specific phobia Others subgroup	Nosemaphobia
Immobility of a joint – fear of developing a 'locked' joint	Specific phobia Others subgroup	Anleylophobia
Imperfection	Specific phobia Others subgroup	Atelophobia

Phobia	Classification	American Name/s
Imprisonment	Specific phobia Others subgroup	Nosemaphobia Nosophobia
Infinity	Specific phobia Others subgroup	Apeirophobia
Injections – sometimes also combined with blood–injury phobia	Specific phobia Blood–injury–injection subgroup	Trypanophobia
Injury – fear of injuring oneself; *see also* accidents	Specific phobia Others subgroup	Traumatophobia
Insanity – fear of losing one's mind or of this condition in others	Specific phobia Others subgroup	Dementophobia Lyssophobia Maniaphobia

Phobia	Classification	American Name/s
Insects	Specific phobia Animals subgroup	Entomophobia Insectophobia
Isolation – fear of being left totally alone, *see also* abandonment	Specific phobia Others subgroup	Isolophobia Monophobia
Itching – especially that caused by biting insects or external parasites	Specific phobia Others subgroup	Acarophobia
Japanese and Japanese culture	Specific phobia Others subgroup	Japanophobia
Jealousy – fear of becoming jealous or of jealousy in others	Specific phobia Others subgroup	Zelophobia
Jews, Jewish customs and religious practices	Specific phobia Others subgroup	Judeophobia

Phobia	Classification	American Name/s
Jumping down from any elevated place	Specific phobia Others subgroup	Catapedaphobia
Kidney disease – fear of developing kidney disease or of this condition in others	Specific phobia Others subgroup Disease phobia	Albuminurophobia
Kissing – fear of kissing or being kissed	Specific phobia Others subgroup	Philemaphobia Philematophobia
Knees	Specific phobia Others subgroup	Genuphobia
Knowledge	Specific phobia Others subgroup	Epistemophobia Gnosiophobia

Phobia	Classification	American Name/s
Lakes	Specific phobia Natural environment subgroup	Limnophobia
Large objects	Specific phobia Others subgroup	Megalophobia
Laughter	Specific phobia Others subgroup	Geliophobia
Lawsuits and legal procedures	Specific phobia Others subgroup	Liticaphobia
Learning	Specific phobia Others subgroup	Sophophobia

Phobia	Classification	American Name/s
Left-handedness – fear of left-handed people	Specific phobia Others subgroup	Sinistrophobia
Left-sidedness – fear of objects on the left side of the person	Specific phobia Others subgroup	Levophobia Sinistrophobia
Leprosy – fear of contracting leprosy, of people with the disease	Specific phobia Others subgroup Disease phobia	Lepraphobia Leprophobia
Lice	Specific phobia Animals subgroup	Pediculophobia Phthiriophobia
Light and bright lights	Specific phobia Others subgroup Photophobia	Photophobia Photoaugliaphobia

Phobia	Classification	American Name/s
Liquids	Specific phobia Others subgroup	Hygrophobia
Loneliness or being alone	Specific phobia Others subgroup	Autophobia Eremophobia
Long waits for an appointment or event	Specific phobia Others subgroup	Macrophobia
Long words	Specific phobia Others subgroup	Sequipedalophobia
Looking up	Specific phobia Others subgroup	Anablephobia
Loud noise	Specific phobia Others subgroup	Ligyrophobia

Phobia	Classification	American Name/s
Love – being in love	Specific phobia Others subgroup	Philophobia
Lovemaking, *see also* sex, coitus	Specific phobia Others subgroup	Malaxophobia Sarmassophobia
Machines	Specific phobia Others subgroup	Mechanophobia
Maggots	Specific phobia Animals subgroup	Scoleciphobia Mathaphobia
Marriage	Specific phobia Others subgroup	Gamophobia

Phobia	Classification	American Name/s
Materialism	Specific phobia Others subgroup	Hylephobia (also used for epilepsy)
Meat	Specific phobia Others subgroup	Carnophobia
Medicines – having to take medicine	Specific phobia Others subgroup	Pharmacophobia
Memories	Specific phobia Others subgroup	Mnemophobia
Men	Specific phobia Others subgroup	Androphobia Arrhenphobia Hominophobia

Phobia	Classification	American Name/s
Menstruation	Specific phobia Others subgroup	Menophobia
Mercury and mercurial substances	Specific phobia Others subgroup	Hydrargyo-phobia
Metals	Specific phobia Others subgroup	Metallophobia
Meteors	Specific phobia Natural environment subgroup	Meteorophobia
Mice	Specific phobia Animals subgroup	Murophobia Musophobia

Phobia	Classification	American Name/s
Mind – fear of the mind and thoughts	Specific phobia Others subgroup	Psychophobia
Mirrors and seeing oneself reflected	Specific phobia Others subgroup	Catoptrophobia Eisoptrophobia
Money	Specific phobia Others subgroup	Chrematophobia Chrometophobia
Monsters – fear or mythical monsters of those created in films, etc	Specific phobia Others subgroup	Teratophobia
Monotony and sameness	Specific phobia Others subgroup	(Homophobia)

Phobia	Classification	American Name/s
Moon	Specific phobia Natural environment subgroup	Selenophobia
Mother-in-law	Specific phobia Others subgroup	Pentheraphobia
Motion and movement	Specific phobia Others subgroup	Kinesophobia Kinetophobia
Moving houses or changing one's life	Specific phobia Others subgroup	Tropophobia
Mushrooms and fungi	Specific phobia Others subgroup	Mycophobia

Phobia	Classification	American Name/s
Music	Specific phobia Others subgroup	Melophobia
Myths, stories and legends	Specific phobia Others subgroup	Mythophobia
Names, sometimes specific names – fear of either hearing or reading a name	Specific phobia Others subgroup	Nomatophobia
Narrow objects and places	Specific phobia Others subgroup	Anginophobia Stenophobia
Needles and pins	Specific phobia Others subgroup	Aichmophobia Belonephobia Enetophobia

Phobia	Classification	American Name/s
Neglect of responsibilities and duties	Specific phobia Others subgroup	Paralipophobia
New drugs	Specific phobia Others subgroup	Neopharmaphobia
New ideas, situations or things; novelty	Specific phobia Others subgroup	Cainophobia Cainotophobia Cenophobia Centophobia Kainolophobia Kainophobia Neophobia
Newspapers	Specific phobia Others subgroup	Graphophobia Cainophobia Papyrophobia

Phobia	Classification	American Name/s
Night – fear of night-time (and darkness)	Specific phobia Natural environment subgroup	Noctiphobia
Nocturnal emission (wet dreams)	Specific phobia Others subgroup	Oneitogmophobia
Noise	Specific phobia Others subgroup	Acousticophobia
Northern Lights	Specific phobia Natural environment subgroup	Auroraphobia
Nosebleeds	Specific phobia Others subgroup	Epistaxiophobia

Phobia	Classification	American Name/s
Nuclear weapons	Specific phobia Others subgroup	Nucleomituphobia
Nudity	Specific phobia Others subgroup	Gymnophobia Nudophobia
Numbers in general and also specific numbers (Number 8) (Number 13)	Specific phobia Others subgroup	Arithmophobia Numerophobia Octophobia Triskaidekaphobia
Obesity	Specific phobia Others subgroup	Obesophobia Pocrescophobia
Odours	Specific phobia Others subgroup	Olfactophobia Osmophobia Osphresiophobia

Phobia	Classification	American Name/s
Old age and growing old	Specific phobia Others subgroup	Gerascophobia Gerontophobia
Old people	Specific phobia Others subgroup	Gerontophobia
Open spaces	Agoraphobia	Agoraphobia
Opening one's eyes	Specific phobia Others subgroup	Optophobia
Operations, the fear of performing operations on the part of a surgeon	Specific phobia Others subgroup	Tomophobia
Opinions – fear of the opinions and criticisms of others, fear of being judged in a negative way	Specific phobia Others subgroup	Allodoxaphobia

Phobia	Classification	American Name/s
Opposite sex	Specific phobia Others subgroup	Heterophobia Sexophobia
Otters	Specific phobia Animals subgroup	Lutraphobia
Overwork – fear of having more work than can be coped with	Specific phobia Others subgroup	Ponophobia
Pain	Specific phobia Others subgroup	Agliophobia Algophobia Odynephobia Odynophobia
Paper	Specific phobia Others subgroup	Papyrophobia

Phobia	Classification	American Name/s
Parasites	Specific phobia Animals subgroup	Parasitophobia
Parents-in-law	Specific phobia Others subgroup	Soceraphobia
Peanut butter clogging up mouth	Specific phobia Others subgroup	Arachibutyrophobia
Pellagra	Specific phobia Others subgroup Disease phobia	Pellagrophobia
Penis – fear of penis, especially erect	Specific phobia Others subgroup	Icthyphallophobia Medorthophobia Phallophobia

Phobia	Classification	American Name/s
People or society	Specific phobia Others subgroup	Anthropophobia Sociophobia
Philosophy and philosophical discussions	Specific phobia Others subgroup	Philosophobia
Phobia itself – fear of becoming phobic	Specific phobia Others subgroup	Phobophobia
Places – fear of specific places	Specific phobia Others subgroup	Topophobia
Plans – fear of making decisive plans	Specific phobia Others subgroup	Teleophobia
Plants	Specific phobia Others subgroup	Batonophobia

Phobia	Classification	American Name/s
Pleasurable feelings	Specific phobia Others subgroup	Hedonophobia
Poetry	Specific phobia Others subgroup	Metrophobia
Pointed objects	Specific phobia Others subgroup	Aichmophobia
Poison and being poisoned or accidentally ingesting poison	Specific phobia Others subgroup	Iophobia Toxicophobia Toxiphobia Toxophobia
Poliomyelitis – fear of contracting polio or of those affected by polio	Specific phobia Others subgroup Disease phobia	Poliosophobia

Phobia		Classification	American Name/s
Politicians		Specific phobia Others subgroup	Politicophobia
Pope – fear of the Pope		Specific phobia Others subgroup	Papaphobia
Poverty		Specific phobia Others subgroup	Peniaphobia
Precipices		Specific phobia Natural environment subgroup	Cremnophobia
Pregnancy (and childbirth)		Specific phobia Others subgroup	Tocophobia

Phobia	Classification	American Name/s
Priests	Specific phobia Others subgroup	Hierophobia
Progress	Specific phobia Others subgroup	Prosophobia
Property	Specific phobia Others subgroup	Orthophobia
Prostitutes	Specific phobia Others subgroup	Cyprianophobia Cypridophobia Cyprinophobia Cypriphobia
Public speaking	Social phobia	Glossophobia Phonophobia

Phobia	Classification	American Name/s
Punishment	Specific phobia Others subgroup	Mastigophobia Poinephobia
Puppets	Specific phobia Others subgroup	Pupaphobia
Purple – the colour purple	Specific phobia Others subgroup	Porphyrophobia
Rabies – fear of contracting rabies	Specific phobia Others subgroup Disease phobia	Cynophobia Hydrophobia Kynophobia
Radiation – fear of being exposed to radiation, x-rays, etc	Specific phobia Others subgroup	Radiophobia

Phobia	Classification	American Name/s
Rain – fear of being out in the rain and rain falling on one's person	Specific phobia Natural environment subgroup	Ombrophobia Pluviophobia
Rape	Specific phobia Others subgroup	Virginitiphobia
Rats	Specific phobia Animals subgroup	Zemmiphobia
Rectum – fear of the rectum and rectal conditions and diseases	Specific phobia Others subgroup	Proctophobia Rectophobia
Red – fear of the colour red	Specific phobia Others subgroup	Ereuthophobia Erythrophobia

Phobia	Classification	American Name/s
Red lights	Specific phobia Others subgroup	Erytophobia
Religion and religious ceremony	Specific phobia Others subgroup	Teleophobia Theophobia
Reptiles	Specific phobia Animals subgroup	Herpetophobia
Responsibility – fear of taking responsibility or being held responsible	Specific phobia Others subgroup	Hypegiaphobia Hypengyophobia
Ridicule – fear of being ridiculed by others or of feeling ridiculous	Social phobia	Catagelophobia Katagelophobia

Phobia	Classification	American Name/s
Right-sidedness – fear of things or objects to the right of the body	Specific phobia Others subgroup	Dextrophobia
Rivers and running water	Specific phobia Natural environment subgroup	Potamophobia
Road travel – fear of all forms of road travel	Specific phobia Situational subgroup	Hodophobia
Robbery – fear of being robbed and of robbers	Specific phobia Others subgroup	Harpaxophobia Scelerophobia
Rods – fear of being beaten with a rod	Specific phobia Others subgroup	Rhabdophobia

Phobia	Classification	American Name/s
Rooms	Specific phobia Situational subgroup	Koinoniphobia
Ruins	Specific phobia Situational subgroup	Atephobia
Russians and Russian culture	Specific phobia Others subgroup	Russophobia
Sacred objects	Specific phobia Others subgroup	Hierophobia
Saints	Specific phobia Others subgroup	Hagiophobia
Scabies	Specific phobia Others subgroup	Scabiophobia

Phobia	Classification	American Name/s
School – fear of going to school	Specific phobia Situational subgroup School phobia	Didaskaleinophobia Scolionophobia
Science	Specific phobia Others subgroup	
Scientific terms	Specific phobia Others subgroup	Hellenologophobia
Scratches – fear of being scratched	Specific phobia Others subgroup	Amychophobia
Sea	Specific phobia Natural environment subgroup	Thalassophobia

Phobia	Classification	American Name/s
Sermons	Specific phobia Others subgroup	Homilophobia
Sexual abuse	Specific phobia Others subgroup	Agraphobia Contreltophobia
Sexual matters – fear of sexual love and contact or any references to these	Specific phobia Others subgroup	Erotophobia Genophobia
Sexual perversion – fear of hearing about or encountering someone who is considered to be perverted or of becoming so oneself	Specific phobia Others subgroup	Paraphobia
Shadows	Specific phobia Others subgroup	Sciaphobia Sciophobia

Phobia	Classification	American Name/s
Shellfish	Specific phobia Animals subgroup	Ostraconophobia
Shock – fear of being shocked, feeling shock	Specific phobia Others subgroup	Hormephobia
Sin – fear of committing an unforgivable sin or sinning	Specific phobia Others subgroup	Enissophobia Enosilphobia Hamartophobia Peccatophobia
Single state – fear of being unmarried	Specific phobia Others subgroup	Anuptaphobia
Sitting – fear of sitting down	Specific phobia Others subgroup	Cathisophobia Kathisophobia Thaasophobia

Phobia	Classification	American Name/s
Skin lesions and skin conditions – fear of these in others or of developing them oneself	Specific phobia Others subgroup Disease phobia	Dermatopathophobia Dermatophobia Dermatosiophobia
Sleep – fear of falling asleep	Specific phobia Others subgroup	Somniphobia
Slime	Specific phobia Others subgroup	Blennophobia Myxophobia
Small objects – fear of very small things	Specific phobia Others subgroup	Microphobia Mycrophobia
Smothering – fear of being smothered or choked	Specific phobia Others subgroup	Pnigerophobia Pnigophobia

Phobia	Classification	American Name/s
Snakes	Specific phobia Animals subgroup	Ophidiophobia Snakephobia
Snow	Specific phobia Others subgroup	Chionophobia
Sourness	Specific phobia Others subgroup	Acerophobia
Space – fear of open space – fear of falling if crossing an open space without means of support	Agoraphobia or Specific phobia Situational subgroup	Cenophobia
Space – fear of outer space	Specific phobia Others subgroup	Astrophobia Spacephobia

Phobia	Classification	American Name/s
Speaking	Specific phobia Others subgroup	Laliophobia Lalophobia
Speaking in public – speech-making	Social phobia	Glossophobia
Speed – fear of anything travelling fast	Specific phobia Others subgroup	Tachophobia
Spiders	Specific phobia Animals subgroup Arachnophobia	Arachnophobia
Stages – fear of stage fright	Social phobia or Specific phobia Situational subgroup	Topophobia

Phobia	Classification	American Name/s
Stairs – fear of going up or down stairs and of falling on stairs	Specific phobia Situational subgroup	Climacophobia
Standing – fear of standing up; fear of being unable to stand	Specific phobia Others subgroup	Basiphobia Basophobia Stasiphobia Strasibasiphobia
Staring – fear of being stared at	Specific phobia Others subgroup	Ophthalmophobia Scopophobia Scoptophobia
Stars	Specific phobia Natural environment subgroup	Astrophobia

Phobia	Classification	American Name/s
Statues	Specific phobia Others subgroup	Automatono-phobia
Stealing – fear that one might steal	Specific phobia Others subgroup	Cleptophobia Kleptophobia
Stepmother	Specific phobia Others subgroup	Novercaphobia
Stepfather	Specific phobia Others subgroup	Vitricophobia
Streets and roads	Specific phobia Situational subgroup	Agyrophobia
Stings – fear of being stung	Specific phobia Others subgroup	Cnidophobia

Phobia	Classification	American Name/s
Stooping – fear of stooped persons or becoming stooped oneself	Specific phobia Others subgroup	Kyphophobia
String(s)	Specific phobia Others subgroup	Cnidophobia Linonophobia
Stuttering – fear of stuttering, especially in front of others or of developing a stutter	Social phobia or Specific phobia Others subgroup	Psellismophobia
Sun – fear of being exposed to the sun	Specific phobia Natural environment subgroup	Heliophobia Photophobia
Swallowing – fear of swallowing or being swallowed	Specific phobia Others subgroup	Phagophobia

119

Phobia	Classification	American Name/s
Symbols and signs	Specific phobia Others subgroup	Symbolophobia
Symmetry – fear of symmetrical things	Specific phobia Others subgroup	Symmetrophobia
Syphilis	Specific phobia Others subgroup Disease phobia	Luiphobia Syphilophobia
Taking tests – fear of having to take any form of test	Specific phobia Others subgroup	Testophobia
Tapeworms	Specific phobia Animals subgroup	Taeniophobia Teniophobia

Phobia	Classification	American Name/s
Tastes – fear of tasting (unpleasant) substances	Specific phobia Others subgroup	Geumaphobia Geumophobia
Technology	Specific phobia Others subgroup	Technophobia
Teeth and dental treatment	Specific phobia Others subgroup Dental phobia	Odontophobia
Termites and other wood-boring or wood-eating insects	Specific phobia Animals subgroup	Isopterophobia
Telephones, also fear of voices on telephones	Specific phobia Others subgroup	Telephonophobia Phonophobia

Phobia	Classification	American Name/s
Tetanus	Specific phobia Others subgroup Disease phobia	Tetanophobia
Theatres	Specific phobia Situational subgroup	Theatrophobia
Theology	Specific phobia Others subgroup	Theologicophobia
Thoughts	Specific phobia Others subgroup	Phronemophobia

Phobia	Classification	American Name/s
Thunder and lightning – fear of storms	Specific phobia Natural environment subgroup Storm phobia	Astraphobia Astropophobia Brontophobia Ceraunophobia Keraunophobia Tonitrophobia
Time – fear of the passage of time	Specific phobia Others subgroup	Chronophobia
Toads	Specific phobia Animals subgroup	Butonophobia
Tombs and tombstones	Specific phobia Situational subgroup	Placophobia

Phobia	Classification	American Name/s
Touching and being touched (being touched)	Specific phobia Others subgroup	Aphenphosmophobia Haphephobia Haptephobia Chiraptophobia
Trains and train travel	Specific phobia Situational subgroup	Siderodromo-phobia
Trees	Specific phobia Situational subgroup	Dendrophobia
Trembling – fear of trembling (itself a symptom of extreme fear)	Specific phobia Others subgroup	Tremophobia
Trichinosis	Specific phobia Others subgroup Disease phobia	Trichinophobia

Phobia	Classification	American Name/s
Tuberculosis	Specific phobia Others subgroup Disease phobia	Phthisiophobia Tuberculophobia
Tyrants – fear of being tyrannised	Specific phobia Others subgroup	Tyrannophobia
Ugliness – fear of being considered ugly or of ugly people and things	Specific phobia Others subgroup	Cacophobia
Undressing – fear of undressing, especially in front of others	Specific phobia Others subgroup	Dishabiliophobia
Urine and urination	Specific phobia Others subgroup	Urophobia

Phobia	Classification	American Name/s
Untidiness	Specific phobia Others subgroup	Ataxophobia
Vaccination	Specific phobia Blood–injury–injection phobia	Vaccinophobia
Vegetables – sometimes specific types	Specific phobia Others subgroup	Lachanophobia
Vehicles	Specific phobia Others subgroup	Ochophobia
Venereal disease	Specific phobia Others subgroup Disease phobia	Cyprianophobia Cypridophobia Cyprinophobia Cypriphobia

Phobia	Classification	American Name/s
Ventriloquist's dummies	Specific phobia Others subgroup	Automatonophobia
Vertigo – especially in connection with height phobia	Specific phobia Others subgroup Height phobia	Illyngophobia
Virgins and young girls	Specific phobia Others subgroup	Parthenophobia
Voids – fear of vast empty rooms	Specific phobia Situational subgroup	Kenophobia
Vomiting – fear of vomiting, especially in a social setting	Social phobia or Specific phobia Others subgroup	Emetophobia

Phobia	Classification	American Name/s
Walking – fear of walking or inability to walk	Specific phobia Others subgroup	Ambulophobia
Walloons	Specific phobia Others subgroup	Walloonphobia
Wasps	Specific phobia Animals subgroup	Spheksophobia
Water (classically applied to that accompanying rabies)	Specific phobia Others subgroup Hydrophobia Water phobia	Hydrophobia
Waves and wavelike movement	Specific phobia Natural environment subgroup	Cymophobia Kymophobia

Phobia	Classification	American Name/s
Waxworks	Specific phobia Others subgroup	Automatono- phobia
Wealth	Specific phobia Others subgroup	Plutophobia
Weight gain	Specific phobia Others subgroup	Obesophobia Pocrescophobia
Whirlpools	Specific phobia Natural environment subgroup	Dinophobia
White – fear of the colour white	Specific phobia Others subgroup	Leukophobia

Phobia	Classification	American Name/s
Wild animals	Specific phobia Animals subgroup	Agrizoophobia
Wind	Specific phobia Natural environment subgroup	Ancraophobia Anemophobia
Wine	Specific phobia Others subgroup	Oenophobia
Witches and witchcraft	Specific phobia Others subgroup	Wiccaphobia
Women	Specific phobia Others subgroup	Gynephobia Gynophobia

Phobia	Classification	American Name/s
Wood and wooden objects	Specific phobia Others subgroup	Xylophobia
Woodlands and forests at night	Specific phobia Natural environment subgroup	Nyctohylophobia
Words – also fear of a particular word, either spoken or in writing	Specific phobia Others subgroup	Logophobia Onomatophobia Verbophobia
Work – or fear of the ability to work or function	Specific phobia Others subgroup	Ergasiophobia Ergophobia
Worms	Specific phobia Animals subgroup	Scoleciphobia

Phobia	Classification	American Name/s
Worm (parasite) infestation	Specific phobia Animals subgroup	Helminthophobia
Wrinkles – fear of becoming lined and wrinkled	Specific phobia Others subgroup	Rhytiphobia
Writing – fear of printed writing	Specific phobia Others subgroup	Graphophobia
Writing in public	Social phobia	Scriptophobia
Yellow – fear of the colour yellow	Specific phobia Others subgroup	Xanthrophobia

Chapter 7
Animal Specific Phobia

Specific phobia

Specific phobia has the following five subgroups:

1.   Animal phobia
2.   Natural environment phobia
3.   Blood–injury–injection phobia
4.   Situational phobia
5.   Other phobias.

The first of these subgroups, animal phobia, forms an extremely important subgroup of specific phobias for several reasons.

Animal specific phobia

Firstly, animal phobias are highly prevalent – studies indicate that about forty per cent of people with a specific phobia are animal phobics. Among this group, by far the most common animal causes of phobic fears are bugs (insects and spiders), snakes, mice and bats, making these the most prevalent of all phobias. (Most readers will, for example, be able to think of at least one person among their family and friends who has a strong aversion to, or fear of, spiders, which may, in some cases, be severe enough to be classed as phobic.)

Animal phobias (particularly the bugs, snakes, mice and bats category), appear to be somewhat more common in women than in men and they arise in early childhood, with the mean age of first appearance being around seven years.

Secondly, the animal subgroup is arguably the most highly studied of all the various types of phobia. It has provided the subject matter for theories about the origins, development, mechanisms and behavioural and cognitive processes that may apply to all phobias. Through increased understanding of these processes and ongoing studies, more sophisticated treatments are continually being evolved and tested which may be beneficial to all phobics and not just those suffering from specific phobias. One of the most promising developments has been the formulation of single-session treatments which have been shown to work especially well for animal phobias.

Symptoms of animal phobia

In common with all other phobias, the animal phobic experiences intense, irrational and unreasonable fear when confronted with his feared subject or can only endure its presence with great difficulty. The fear may produce physiological responses or induce symptoms of panic. The nature of the fear in animal phobia has been the subject of intense study and several factors appear to have emerged. Irrespective of the initial reasons behind the development of the phobia, the fear appears to be related to a series of (mistaken) negative beliefs (cognitive factors) that interact with each other. These are:

- beliefs concerning the animal itself and the harm it is able to cause the person, either through some form of attack or through other means such as disease or contamination.
- beliefs about the consequences for the person as a result of the encounter, that is that he will lose physical and/or mental control and become helpless, have a panic attack or faint. The person believes that these responses will be extremely awful for him and this can heighten his anxiety and physiological responses which then feed each other. From the phobic point of view, any of these outcomes would make it easier for an animal to attack so it can be easily seen that these beliefs maintain each other.
- beliefs that, if confronted with the animal, the person will be trapped and not be able to find a means of escape, either in the actual physical sense or because of his helplessness and inability to cope or to function. It appears that the greater the degree of disbelief concerning one's ability to cope, the higher the likelihood of phobic avoidance.

Development of animal phobia

Studies of historical writings, particularly those of the doctors and scientists of Ancient Greece and Rome, reveal that animal phobias have afflicted mankind for a very long time and references continue to be made occasionally throughout the succeeding centuries. However, animal phobias only began to attract serious scientific and medical attention in the nineteenth and twentieth centuries and they continue to be the subject of study and debate at the present time.

As with all cases of phobia, avoidance is a key feature of animal phobias but the extent to which this interferes with normal life very much depends upon the prevalence of the feared subject. For example, a snake phobic living in Britain is probably only slightly inconvenienced by his phobia. Native wild snakes are rarely seen in Britain, even by country dwellers, and although the keeping of reptiles as pets has become increasingly popular, it is relatively easy to avoid chance encounters with snakes. Mice and bats are more commonly seen but even they are more likely to be an occasional, rather than an everyday experience for most people.

However, birds, bugs, spiders, dogs and cats are certainly frequently encountered, and it can be envisaged that trying to avoid chance meetings with any of these could significantly affect normal life. As has been discussed elsewhere, avoidance behaviour (safety behaviour at its most extreme) preserves the person from the highly unpleasant experience of fear but it also prevents any possibility of challenging or curing the phobia.

Chapter 8
Animal Specific Phobia:
Spider Phobia

Spider phobia is one of the most common types of animal phobia and usually arises in childhood before the age of ten years. Although it has been intensively studied and many theories about the underlying mechanisms have been put forward, few undisputed facts have emerged. However, two factors concerning the physical characteristics of spiders seem to be relevant and these are the way the animal moves, especially the unpredictability of its movement, and its appearance.

Symptoms of spider phobia

There has been considerable debate about the role of the emotional responses of disgust or revulsion in the acquisition and maintenance of animal phobias. This has been studied in relation to spider phobia but while some experts have produced results which indicate that disgust is relevant, others believe that it is not.

It is interesting to note that anecdotal evidence suggests that many people who are not truly phobic dislike spiders, find them repulsive and have difficulty handling them without the aid of a glove or a piece of kitchen paper.

137

People frequently perceive spiders to be ugly compared to, for example, butterflies which are more likely to be considered colourful and beautiful (although butterflies can also be the subject of phobias). This might suggest that emotional responses to spiders are relevant for some phobics, even if they are not the main factor at work in the phobia.

Development of spider phobia

The development and acquisition of phobias is discussed in Chapter 21 but it is worth commenting here on the role of adverse experiences in spider phobia, sometimes called 'conditioning'. An adverse experience can be briefly described as some kind of direct, one-off first encounter with the animal (stimulus) in which the person became very frightened. In animal phobias, these experiences usually take place in childhood. A number of surveys of spider phobics have been carried out and, while numbers vary, only some of those surveyed are able to remember a particularly bad experience with a spider. A smaller number report vicarious conditioning (observing parents, family or friends being fearful of spiders). Quite frequently, no conditioning experience can be brought to mind and the person states that he has had the phobia for as long as he can remember.

Treatment of spider phobia

As noted in the general discussion about animal phobias, the most important features maintaining the fear of a spider phobic are his mistaken beliefs (cognitive factors) which interact and reinforce one another. These concern his beliefs about how a spider behaves, the harm or damage he will sustain if he is confronted with the animal and whether he will be able to cope or to escape. The person may fear that he will lose physical and mental control, become hysterical, have a panic attack or experience so great a level of anxiety that it will cause a heart attack from which he may die.

Hence modern treatments aim to challenge and to change all the erroneous assumptions of the spider phobic (and in so doing diminish or banish the phobia) by means of a combination of cognitive therapy and behaviour therapy, cognitive–behavioural therapy (*see* page 234).

Cognitive–behavioural treatments for spider phobia consists of three main elements:

- discussion and information-sharing
- modelling
- gradually increased exposure, ending with the patient being comfortably able to handle spiders.

Discussion and information-sharing

The discussion and information aspect includes, firstly, an initial interview with the patient. The aim of this is to discover the exact nature of his beliefs with regard to spiders and how he responds to them, both in a behavioural and in a physiological sense (for example, whether he experiences symptoms of panic).

Next, the exact nature of all these aspects is examined and discussed in detail and the patient is encouraged by the therapist to challenge them in an intellectual sense by being prepared to look at them in a new light. Secondly, the discussion moves on to an explanation of what will happen during treatment and the goals that the patient, with the aid of the therapist, can expect to achieve. It is very important for the full co-operation and consent of the patient to be obtained at this stage and this usually involves a thorough examination of his individual worries concerning treatment and his ability to cope. The second and third elements concern the treatment session itself.

Modelling

Modelling refers to the way in which a therapist first carries out a procedure himself while the patient watches, that is he 'models' the process in order to demonstrate how it can be achieved. The therapist then helps the patient to carry out the procedure himself. In the case of spider phobia, modelling usually involves some form of indirect or direct contact with a spider.

Gradually increased or graded exposure

Gradually increased or graded exposure refers to a series of stages in which contact with a spider is

140

intensified in a carefully planned, controlled way. The patient must be able to comfortably complete one stage (usually several times), with a reduced level of anxiety before progressing to further, more intensive degrees of exposure. Some therapists have refined the technique to such an extent that they are able to offer treatment in one session lasting up to three hours.

However, those who practise this method emphasise that it should be regarded as a starting point for ongoing self-help measures. Often, the treatment session is recorded on video tape and playing the video can form part of the self-help programme as the person is able to remind himself at any time of just how much he has achieved. Thereafter, the most important aspect of self-help is to no longer avoid spiders or the places where they may occur and to become the member of the family who is always asked to put them out of the house.

Chapter 9
Single-session Treatment
for Spider Phobia

Phobia treatments are covered in general terms in a later chapter of this book. However, it is appropriate to describe in detail here the single-session treatment approach to spider therapy as an illustration of the method as a whole.

As mentioned above, the initial stage (which may be the first contact between therapist and patient), is an interview lasting for about one hour in which the exact nature of the individual's phobic beliefs and behaviours are ascertained.

This may be called the 'behavioural analysis interview' and through it the therapist gains valuable insights that enable him to 'tailor' his pre-therapy information and instructions, and the treatment itself, in a manner appropriate to the individual.

Depending upon the amount of time available, there may be a discussion in which the patient's distorted beliefs about spiders and his own abilities to cope begin to be challenged, with the aims of treatment being introduced. It is very important that therapist and patient build up a relationship that enables them to work as a team if treatment is to be successful, so this discussion has to be handled in a careful and expert manner.

The next stage is a 'pre-treatment discussion' in which these factors are more fully explored and the patient is informed about what will take place during treatment itself. This discussion has to address three key issues, namely:

- allay the fears that a patient usually has concerning the treatment.
- ensure that the patient fully understands the concept of graded exposure and the tasks that he and the therapist will undertake together. Also, to ensure that the *goal* of treatment is explained and understood, which is usually for the patient to be able to catch a spider using a glass and a piece of card and put it outside. The person should be able to do this in everyday life without the aid of anyone else.
- make sure that the patient fully understands that he must work and co-operate with, and trust, the therapist and that he is an equal half of the team. Having accepted this responsibility, the patient is asked to commit himself to the treatment session.

Allaying fears of phobic person

Characteristically, a spider phobic has two types of anxiety concerning treatment. Firstly, the person is often concerned that 'shock tactics' will be applied such as being locked into a room full of spiders or having one suddenly thrown at him. The importance of a good relationship between patient and therapist is obvious here. The patient has to be able to believe and trust in the therapist's assurances that this will *never* happen and that everything that occurs during treatment is fully planned and only proceeds with his consent.

Secondly, the spider phobic is often concerned about the high level of anxiety that he will endure during treatment and that he will 'go to pieces', not be able to cope or even have a heart attack. The therapist may challenge this on an intellectual or medical level by trying to help the patient understand that although panic symptoms feel terrible, they are not physically harmful.

However, a different approach is sometimes taken, which is to ask the person to remember the very worst experience of fear that he has had in relation to spiders. He is asked to consider his fear of spiders in terms of a scale ranging from 1 to 100 of Subjective Units of Disturbances (SUDs). His most terrifying experience is rated as 100 SUDs. The therapist then explains that the 100 SUDs rating took place in an uncontrolled, real-life, unplanned exposure to a spider or spiders. In contrast, treatment is carefully planned with the patient himself being in control and consenting to everything that happens. Hence the person's SUDs rate during treatment is bound to be lower than in his worst-case experience which he did, in fact, survive. In this way, the patient is instructed and encouraged to believe that although he may experience anxiety, it will not be beyond his ability to cope. Also, the patient may be told that banishing all anxiety is not the goal of treatment but that a great reduction will inevitably occur as a by-product of successfully completing the treatment.

Explaining graded exposure and the goals of treatment to the phobic person

Although the principle of graded exposure is relatively easy to explain, the therapist may not reveal the more advanced stages in all their detail. This is because until the person begins the treatment process and successfully completes each stage, he finds it hard to accept that he can do this – in other words, treatment is necessary for belief change to take place.

The same holds true for explanations about the goals of treatment. The patient will certainly be informed that his personal goal is to be able to catch a spider with a glass and postcard and put it outside. He is unlikely to be told that the therapist's aim, at the end of the treatment session, is for the patient to be able to have one or two spiders crawling on him, either out of sight or on his hands.

Withholding information, if it occurs, is felt to be justified for two reasons. Firstly, the patient would probably not consent to treatment at all if he knew about this end goal and hence could not be helped to overcome his phobia. Secondly, the person's anxiety level would be greatly raised and his thoughts would be centred on the end goal, even during the early stages of graded exposure. This would interfere with his ability to carry out the treatment tasks and reduce the chance of a successful outcome.

It is important to remember that treatment for spider phobia is highly successful and that a sufferer is normally very pleased and grateful for the result. Hence in this case, the ends could be said to justify the means.

Explaining the 'teamwork' approach

The therapist makes sure that the person fully understands the concept of modelling and that nothing occurs without his full consent and co-operation. Emphasis is laid on the fact that treatment consists of a partnership between therapist and patient. Once both parties are satisfied that everything has been fully discussed and understood, the patient is asked to agree to go ahead with treatment. Immediately before the start of treatment, the patient is asked to describe to the therapist what is about to happen – as a final safeguard to ensure that there is no residual misunderstanding.

Discussion also takes place throughout treatment in order to monitor how the person's beliefs, emotions and anxiety levels are changing. Usually spiders of different sizes are used. The smallest spider is placed in a large, clear plastic bowl and the therapist demonstrates how to catch it using a glass and a piece of card. The patient is then asked to perform this task himself, with the guidance of the therapist.

The process is usually repeated several times until the person feels comfortable about carrying it out. On the final occasion, the patient may be asked to hold the glass quite close to his body or face, examine the spider and describe it as though to someone who had been blind from birth. Doing this generally results in a lessening of fear.

The spider is then returned to the bowl and the patient is asked what he thinks it would do if he put his hand into the container. Almost invariably, the person believes that the spider will make a run for his hand, climb up his arm and disappear beneath his clothes. The therapist then demonstrates that this is not how a spider behaves by touching the animal gently with his finger. In fact, the spider either runs away or freezes and, if the process is repeated, it rapidly gives up and becomes tired.

The next step is to ask the patient to touch the spider. This is necessary in order to demonstrate that it will not behave any differently towards him and to begin to challenge his mistaken phobic beliefs concerning spiders. Achieving this may first require that the patient touches the spider with a pen or pencil, guided by the therapist's hand. The patient is able to see for himself that the spider runs away or becomes tired and he repeats the process until he feels comfortable about doing it and his anxiety decreases. When he feels ready, he is asked to touch the spider, first with the gentle guidance of the therapist's hand and then on his own.

Once again, the patient is usually amazed to discover that the spider has no interest in crawling onto him and just wishes to be left in peace. The next stage is the hardest from the patient's point of view as it involves taking the spider out of its container and allowing it to walk across the hands. This is first demonstrated by the therapist, who lets the spider walk from one of his hands to the other and shows that he can control the speed of its movement. With the therapist's support, the patient is encouraged to place a finger, knuckle side down, on the therapist's palm and allow the spider to walk over it and when this has been comfortably achieved more fingers are gradually put down.

Eventually, the patient is able to allow the spider to walk across his whole hand and back onto the therapist's hand. Then, when he feels ready, he is encouraged to allow it to walk across both his hands, first with the help of the therapist and then on his own. Next, the therapist demonstrates that if the spider is allowed to walk from the palm of one hand to the elbow, its direction can still be controlled with the other hand and it will not disappear beneath clothing. The patient is now asked to prove this for himself, first with guidance and then on his own.

All these stages are then repeated using each of the larger spiders in turn and taking as much time as is necessary. By the end of the session, the person is able to comfortably handle spiders with little or no fear, to the degree that he is able to allow one to crawl upon him out of sight. Or, he can permit two to walk across his hands at the same time. He has achieved much more than the stated goal of being able to catch a spider with a glass. His phobic fear has decreased dramatically and he no longer harbours misplaced beliefs about spiders or catastrophic thoughts concerning encounters with them. With the aid of a video recording of the session, the person is able to put into practice in everyday situations what he has learned during treatment.

Chapter 10
Animal Specific Phobia:
Dog Phobia

Dog phobia is one of a range of relatively common animal phobias which is usually acquired in childhood before the age of ten years. A slight fear of dogs is not uncommon in young children and is understandable in that large, boisterous dogs, even those that are friendly, must seem physically overwhelming to someone small. However, most children lose their nervousness as they grow older and gain more experience of dogs.

Symptoms of dog phobia

As in other animal phobias, phobics experience extreme and irrational fear in relation to dogs. This is an obvious disadvantage in everyday life since these animals are commonly encountered in almost every country of the world. It is probable that most people in the British Isles could expect to encounter a dog at some stage upon leaving their own home and garden, if not every day, then at least fairly frequently. Hence it is easy to appreciate that dog phobia can cause considerable distress. As in other animal phobias, the condition tends to be long-lasting and persistent but is amenable to treatment in most cases.

Development of dog phobia

Studies have shown that at least one half to two thirds of dog phobics can remember a frightening, and usually painful, event as the trigger for their phobia. However, among control groups of non-phobics, a similar number can *also* recall a bad experience with a dog. Almost invariably, it involved being hurt in some way, either being bitten, scratched or knocked over.

The difference between the two groups seems to lie in their expectations regarding chance meetings with dogs. The phobics invariably expect to experience extreme fear or panic and physical harm in the form of attack. In spite of any previous bad encounters, non-dog phobics do not expect such responses or outcomes in chance meetings, although a small minority may admit to feeling some degree of tension, depending upon individual circumstances such as the nature of a particular dog.

Hence it appears that, once again, it is the dog phobic's expectations and beliefs that maintain the phobia. Also, as in spider phobia, these expectations and beliefs fall into the two categories of the phobic's own anticipated and former experience of fear, panic, distress and inability to cope along with his expectation of physical harm from the dog itself. The manner in which a dog moves, its appearance, barking and growling and the way it feels to touch are other factors involved in the phobia.

Treatment of dog phobia

Graduated exposure is the treatment of choice for dog phobia and it can be undertaken in single or multi-session form or as a self-help programme. However, it is essential that the dogs chosen to take part in the treatment are well-behaved and friendly and can be trusted never to act in an aggressive manner. It is well known that domestic animals are highly sensitive and can detect fear in humans. Fear may make a timid dog act in a seemingly aggressive way as a defensive mechanism – barking, raised body hair, cowering with the tail between the legs – and all this appears anything but friendly.

It is evident that a phobic person first needs to become comfortable in the company of quiet and well-behaved dogs in order for fear to diminish. Once this has been achieved, the person is better placed to cope with chance encounters with dogs. He can, for example, learn that usually dogs out on a walk will either ignore him completely or only approach a stranger if they are friendly and sociable. More alarming encounters almost always take the form of a dog barking continuously because it is fearful itself. It is generally unnecessary to approach such a dog but the person can be taught to assume non-threatening 'body language' such as avoiding direct eye contact with the animal.

Experiencing a direct physical attack by a dog is fortunately not common but, as the phobic person may have already discovered, it cannot ever be entirely ruled out. The aim of treatment should be to enable the phobic person to cope with ordinary, everyday encounters with dogs with little or no anxiety. Being taught to understand the behaviour of dogs and how to modify his own behaviour if necessary, lessens the risk of an unpleasant experience and gives the person increased confidence.

Chapter 11
Natural Environment
Specific Phobia

Facts and figures about natural environment phobia are difficult to come by and this particular subgroup is perhaps less amenable to study in that patients with natural environment phobias do not often seek treatment. It appears that much of the knowledge in relation to this group is conjectural rather than factual. For example, it is common for young children to fear the crashes and flashes of a thunderstorm, especially at night, and to seek the safety of their parents' bed. However, while many will grow out of these fears, the number of children who go on to develop storm phobia is not known. Also, it is more common for storm phobia to develop at an older age.

Symptoms of natural environment phobia

Specific phobias involving the natural environment form a broad group encompassing a wide range of phobic stimuli. These include landscape features such as forests and woodlands, caves and caverns and also natural water – the sea, lakes, rivers, waterfalls, whirlpools, etc. A further category includes climatic or weather phenomena such as storms (thunder and lightning), fog, rain, hail or snow. It is possible for almost any feature of the natural environment to be the subject of phobic fear, especially among children.

Development of natural environment phobia

Consideration of natural environment phobias invites a closer look at two aspects: the nature of the phobic fear and the reasons behind the *development* of these phobias. A key factor in phobia is that the fear induced is irrational and out of proportion to any danger presented by the stimulus.

However, it cannot be denied that some natural environment phenomena that can be the cause of phobia *are* dangerous and hence some degree of fear seems understandable. The obvious candidate is a storm involving forked lightning. Although thankfully a rare event, someone is killed in Britain due to a direct lightning strike nearly every year, while others may suffer death or injury indirectly through trees or parts of buildings being struck and falling on them. Knowing these dangers, very few people would choose to remain in the open during a storm and would admit to feeling some degree of apprehension in such circumstances.

Equally, being apprehensive or slightly fearful of the sea, especially during rough weather, is understandable since one's chances of survival, on accidentally falling in, are minimal. In addition, very many people experience similar apprehensive feelings in fog or walking through a dark forest, especially if they are alone. Here, the fear may be of some unknown danger that could be lurking out of sight in the fog or in the forest.

The fact that all these fears are recognised to be a common feature of human experience has been thoroughly exploited by film makers. No doubt every reader can think of examples of horror or thriller films where storms, fog, dark forests and raging seas (along with suitably atmospheric music) have been used to provoke the screams of the audience. Phobic fear is, of course, much more intense, severe and distressing than the fear described above, but in relation to natural environment phobias, it is easy to understand how the low-level anxiety that is commonly experienced might, for some reason, become a disproportionate phobic fear in some people.

Natural environment phobias seem to lend themselves, at least superficially, to some of the current *developmental* theories and models believed to be relevant in the acquisition of phobias. These are described in detail in Chapter 21 although it is probable that, as with most phobias, there are several factors at work.

Treatment of natural environment phobia

People with natural environment phobias very often do not seek treatment and cope by avoiding the feared stimulus. When treatment is needed, graduated exposure is the preferred option although it is unlikely that this can be carried out in a clinical setting. A therapist may be able to use films of, for example, a thunderstorm to try and ascertain and challenge the person's beliefs about storms. Obviously, however, a real thunderstorm cannot be arranged and probably the best that can be done is to discuss a self-help programme that the person can implement the next time that there is a storm. If the feared feature is accessible, such as in the case of a forest, a self-help programme of gradually increased exposure is possible, perhaps enlisting the help of a family member or friend.

Chapter 12
Blood–Injury–Injection
Specific Phobia

Studies have indicated that a high proportion of blood–injury phobics (about seventy per cent) also suffer from injection phobia. However, a lower number of those who have injection phobia as their primary problem additionally report blood–injury phobia (about thirty-one per cent). Hence, although injection phobia can exist alone, it is quite common for it to be associated with blood–injury phobia. Also the majority of people with blood–injury phobia also have injection phobia as part of their condition. It can be readily appreciated that blood–injury–injection phobia has a significant and potentially dangerous effect on normal life.

Symptoms of blood–injury–injection phobia

People with blood–injury phobias suffer extreme anxiety at the sight of blood. The anxiety is triggered not only if they happen to witness a person suffering an accidental injury but also in the controlled environment of someone giving a blood sample or donation or undergoing a surgical procedure. The fear is similarly acute if the person who is bleeding is the phobic himself and people with this phobia are overly anxious at the thought of sustaining an injury. Injection phobics find it impossible to undergo any medical procedure that involves the insertion of a surgical needle because of their extreme fear and they have great difficulty in seeing this happen to anyone else. Routine immunisations and minor surgical procedures are feared and avoided and the phobic person may even refuse treatment that is needed for an underlying medical problem. Not only this, the phobic person characteristically experiences considerable anxiety outwith the phobic situation in relation to his perceived inability to come to the aid of a person who is hurt. This anxiety is particularly acute if the phobic person has young children who would be reliant upon him for help.

In addition, blood–injury–injection phobics worry about being unable to safeguard their health. Some never visit their doctor even if they have health concerns. Others completely avoid hospitals, even to visit a sick relative or friend, or do not watch television or films for fear of seeing images of injured people. A small proportion of women are afraid to become pregnant because of their phobia. Hence, in contrast to some other types of specific phobia, simply avoiding the feared situation is not enough to banish anxiety and enable the person to lead a normal life.

Fainting – a unique characteristic of BII phobia

A more or less unique characteristic of blood–injury–injection phobia is the high incidence of fainting experienced by sufferers upon exposure to the feared stimulus. In any particular BII phobic sample, seventy per cent, or more, of the sufferers report fainting, which has usually occurred several times. In medical terms, this type of response is known as vasovagal syncope or 'emotional fainting' and it occurs as a result of reflex-like activity in the parasympathetic nervous system.

In essence, electrical activity in the parasympathetic fibres of the vagus nerve which supply the heart causes bradycardia (a fall in heartbeat rate), hypotension (a lowering of blood pressure), cerebral ischaemia and hypoxia (a lessening of the blood supply to the brain and consequent momentary lack of oxygen), all of which results in a brief loss of consciousness. In a small number of people, periods of cardiac asystole (no electrical output from the heart recorded on an ECG) lasting several seconds have been reported during the faint.

Emotional fainting is in marked contrast to the physiological reaction experienced by most specific phobia suffers. This consists of a heightened response in the sympathetic nervous system that causes tachycardia (an increased heartbeat rate) and hypertension (raised blood pressure), along with a range of other possible symptoms of fear.

Studies usually reveal a high incidence of fainting (seventy per cent or greater) among blood–injury–injection phobics during exposure to the feared stimulus. However, it is interesting to note that fainting is also quite common among blood donors who are not known to be phobic, the rate running at about five per cent of those who give blood. Readers who are blood donors will know that they are monitored for signs of fainting after donation. However, there is no good medical reason why fainting should occur.

Also, emotional fainting, and even cardiac asystole, have been reported during other medical procedures. Under these circumstances, it usually occurs during procedures that are invasive such as dilation of the cervix in women, rectal examination of the prostate gland in men and insertion of a cardiac catheter.

Also, fainting may occur unexpectedly in other situations such as sudden emptying of the bladder (especially in men during the night), standing up too quickly and prolonged standing and placing the face under water.

Two other aspects of blood–injury–injection phobia seem especially interesting. Firstly, very many people with this phobia have a close family member who is also affected, leading some experts to believe that there is a genetic factor at work.

Secondly, the emotional responses of aversion and revulsion may be involved and it has been suggested that a heightened sense of disgust may be partly responsible for activating the parasympathetic

161

responses that lead to emotional fainting, although further research is needed for confirmation.

However, in this context it is relevant to note that many people who are not truly phobic experience revulsion and some degree of anxiety at the sight of blood, especially if the source is a person who is injured, hurt and bleeding. Those affected may try to avoid watching graphic depictions of violence and catastrophe on television or on films because they feel disturbed by the images and find it hard to banish them from their minds. Such responses are frequently reported in both children and adults and hence it would appear that blood–injury–injection phobias represent the extreme end of a spectrum of common human fears.

Diagnosis of blood–injury–injection phobia

In order to diagnose blood–injury–injection phobia, a preliminary interview takes place in which the person is asked a series of questions about their condition. The questions cover the nature of the fear experienced in relation to particular circumstances, whether the person faints or nearly faints, the degree of avoidance and the extent to which normal life is disrupted.

In some clinics, a standardised set of questions (which the person answers as True or False) is used called 'The Mutilation Questionnaire'. If the answers indicate a positive diagnosis, some clinics conduct an 'exposure test' based upon the showing of a colour video depicting surgery and/or people having injections or giving blood. The purpose is to evaluate the person's physiological and behavioural reactions and to question them about their feelings of anxiety while the tape is being shown. The test is carried out with the full consent of the person who is thoroughly briefed beforehand about the contents of the video.

The patient is asked to keep his eyes on the screen but is given the remote control unit so that he can stop the film at any time if watching it becomes intolerable. His blood pressure and heartbeat rate are monitored continuously throughout the process (and other signs are noted), beginning with a ten-minute pre-exposure phase in which baseline readings are obtained. A four-minute instruction period follows during which the person is reminded about the contents of the video and is asked to watch the screen without looking away. The video lasts for half an hour and, usually, a phobic person either faints, looks away or stops the tape because of marked anxiety and distress.

Development of blood–injury–injection phobia

Studies have shown that blood–injury–injection phobias are normally acquired in childhood or in the teenage years (with the peak age at around eight or nine) and they continue, if not treated, into adult life.

It is uncommon for people to acquire these phobias for the first time in adulthood. Very few studies have examined the part played by adverse experiences in the acquisition of blood–injury–injection phobias. Those that have been carried out indicate that a little over half of BII phobics report a direct traumatic incident involving themselves, as the trigger for their phobia. A further quarter recall vicarious or indirect conditioning (such as seeing someone else experiencing a BII phobic episode) while most of the remainder cannot remember any particular conditions attached to the onset of their phobia. In general, most of the group who do not report either a direct or indirect conditioning experience are unable to recall the start of their phobia and state that it has existed for as long as they can remember. These findings are reasonably consistent with those that have been reported for some other specific phobias.

In common with other types of specific phobia, blood–injury–injection phobics have negative beliefs connected with their phobia and not surprisingly, most of these concern fainting and its possible consequences. Most people who have experienced fainting or feeling faint regard it as an unpleasant physical experience and it may be preceded by a feeling of light-headedness, sweating, nausea and visual and auditory disturbance. In spite of the fact that the body of a person who faints is usually totally relaxed and does not sustain lasting injury, bruising may occur or, rarely, a limb or the head may be struck as a result of collapse. Following a faint, a person may experience momentary confusion but normally recovers rapidly, although it is common for there to be some residual feelings of unease.

For all these reasons, it is perhaps not surprising that BII phobics fear the fainting which is so highly associated with their condition. Indeed, it has been suggested that to define this fear as 'unreasonable' or 'excessive' (as laid down in the criteria for definition of phobia) is possibly less applicable in the case of blood–injury–injection phobia.

People with other phobias who suffer from panic symptoms also experience unpleasant physical symptoms and they frequently believe that these indicate the presence of an organic disease. However, panic symptoms are not, in fact, physically harmful in any way. In contrast, it is well-known that fainting may sometimes be symptomatic of an underlying disease or condition so one might expect that BII phobics who fainted would be inclined to believe that they were physically ill. There is, however, no reliable evidence that this is a prevalent view and most BII phobics appear to firmly associate their fainting with the phobic stimulus alone.

Treatment of blood–injury–injection phobia

Since fainting is so prevalent in this category of specific phobia, treatment has two purposes that must be addressed simultaneously. These are to reverse the physiological processes that lead to fainting while, at the same time, reducing and hopefully eliminating the fear caused by the phobic stimulus. Classic graduated exposure therapy has been shown to help some patients.

In the case of blood–injury phobics, slides and video films would normally be used, possibly along with surgical instruments. For injection phobia, slides and films along with surgical needles can be employed to gradually increase the degree of exposure. In both instances, the patient usually starts by lying down to reduce the risk of fainting and then gradually progresses to sitting and standing as treatment continues.

Recently, a new approach has been developed by a group of Swedish clinicians which has proved successful and teaches the patient a method of preventing fainting. The technique is called 'Applied Tension' and, in essence, the person is taught how to tense the large body muscles for short periods of time (fifteen to twenty seconds) which has the effect of raising blood pressure and heartbeat rate. By being able to directly influence his own blood pressure, the patient is able to counteract the hypotension that is the usual precursor of vasovagal syncope.

In order for the process to be successful, several aspects have to be addressed. One of the most important is to ensure that the person understands the reasons why he faints and the physiological processes that take place, which can be counteracted by applied tension. Secondly, the patient has to be taught to recognise the very first signs of faintness that he experiences (such as sweating, queasy feelings or nausea, sight and hearing disturbances) so that he knows when to begin applied tension. Thirdly, he needs to be instructed in applied tension and the therapist must ensure that the patient feels comfortable with the procedure and is able to perform it correctly.

The patient then applies the technique during treatment sessions which begin by using slides and films during which the person's blood pressure and heartbeat rate are monitored and he is questioned about his feelings and beliefs. However, by the fourth treatment session, the blood–injury phobic is able to witness the procedures at a blood donor centre and in the fifth and final one, to watch thoracic surgery. By the end of treatment, injection phobics are able to undergo finger pricking, injections and venipuncture and feel comfortable in the presence of needles and surgical instruments. The method has proved to be helpful to many blood–injury–injection phobics and has been further refined and applied as a single-session treatment (*see* Chapter 9).

Chapter 13
Situational Specific Phobia:
Claustrophobia

In common with natural environment phobias, facts and figures about situational specific phobias as a whole are hard to come by. The group tends to be defined by its best-studied examples which include claustrophobia (*see* page 169), flying or flight phobia (*see* page 179), bridge phobia, and accident phobia (*see* page 183).

Symptoms of situational phobia

As the name implies, people suffering from this subgroup of specific phobias experience extreme fear if they are exposed to a particular situation or set of circumstances. Although the situation may form part of the man-made environment, this is not always the case and there is some degree of overlap with the natural environment subgroup of specific phobias.

However, one or two interesting aspects appear to emerge. Firstly, as revealed by the phobias list, a wide range of stimuli can provoke situational phobias. However, while some stimuli are quite limited (for example, crossing bridges and flying), others are more broadly based as in claustrophobia.

Secondly, while it is possible for almost any situation

to be the source of phobic fear, most are thought to be uncommon. The true incidence is difficult to determine since most people whose phobias fall into this subgroup do not come forward for treatment and cope by avoiding the feared situation. Even in the better known examples of claustrophobia and flying phobia, it is thought that very few people seek professional help. Those who do are usually motivated to do so because the phobia is interfering significantly with normal life, often making it difficult for them to meet work commitments.

Claustrophobia is explored in this chapter and flying phobia and accident phobia in the next two chapters.

Symptoms of claustrophobia

Claustrophobia is a relatively common condition which is classically defined as an intense fear of being in a small, shut-in or confined space (from the Latin, *claustrum*, meaning an enclosed space). Surveys indicate that it affects between two and five per cent of the population at any one time, most commonly in the age group between eighteen and twenty-five years, although it may appear in childhood. Also, it is more prevalent in females than in males and is among the 'top ten' of the most commonly recorded phobias.

Very few sufferers seek help for their condition and it is believed that this is partly because many are unaware of the effective treatment that is available.

Victims cope by avoiding feared situations that may cause significant inconvenience, particularly if their claustrophobia is experienced in response to a broad range of stimuli. However, it can be difficult to completely avoid claustrophobic situations and the degree of distress endured by sufferers can be considerable. In some instances, the phobia can have potentially more serious consequences as, for example, in the case of a person who needs a diagnostic medical imaging scan, but is unable to undergo the procedure because of his inability to endure being enclosed within the machine.

Questioning claustrophobics about the nature of their fear does not usually provide satisfactory answers. Sufferers are often puzzled themselves about what exactly frightens them or what they think will happen to them. However, detailed studies of claustrophobia have revealed that it is a complex condition in which two aspects combine to maintain fear. These are:

- the element of physical restriction and being trapped
- the belief that, in a small space, the air supply is insufficient and suffocation will ensue.

Fear of physical restriction and being trapped

Most people feel uncomfortable if their movement is restricted, even if the circumstances present no danger at all. Signs of this anxiety are frequently seen in domestic mammals that are confined or restrained but in wild animals, the fear can be extreme and even result in stress-induced, sudden death. In claustrophobics, the stress or fear response provoked by any form of physical restriction is highly developed.

This helps to explain why people with this condition experience phobic fear not only in small, confined spaces such as a lift, phone box or cubicle of a public toilet but also in other, less obvious, circumstances, such as sitting in a chair at the hairdresser or in a seat on public transport, waiting in a supermarket queue or being among a crowd of people.

This aspect of claustrophobia provides evident similarities with agoraphobia in which feelings of being trapped and inability to escape to safety are a prominent feature.

Fear of suffocation in small, confined spaces

A belief that they will suffocate in a confined space is reported by a majority of claustrophobics. In real life, suffocation can only take place in three circumstances:

- if air or oxygen is used up
- if a person has a severe respiratory disorder, serious asthma attack or extreme allergic reaction (anaphylaxis)
- if the person's breathing is physically restricted, for example, by smothering.

171

Suffocation when air or oxygen is used up

In relation to the first circumstances, it is interesting to note that studies indicate that there are widely held, popular misconceptions regarding the amount of air a person requires to survive in a confined space. The majority of people greatly overestimate the amount of air that is needed to survive in, for example, an airtight room and underestimate how long this air would last, believing that they would be in immediate danger of deprivation. In fact, it is usually possible to survive for days rather than hours, allowing rescue to take place in most circumstances. In the majority of cases, a confined space is not sealed and yet the mistaken belief that the air supply is threatened persists. Hence, it has been suggested that this general belief contributes to the fear in claustrophobia.

Suffocation through a severe respiratory disorder, serious asthma attack or extreme allergic reaction (anaphylaxis)

Turning to the second circumstance, it is apparent that the majority of claustrophobics do not suffer from physical disorders that restrict normal breathing. Significantly, however, very many of them report fear-induced physical symptoms in the phobic situation, or panic, of which the major components are breathlessness and feelings of being smothered. Also, chest pain or tightness, choking, dizziness and a feeling of being about to faint are commonly experienced. Even among claustrophobics who do not suffer such extreme symptoms, a raised heartbeat rate and hyperventilation are usually reported.

It is possible that the claustrophobic belief in suffocation may partly arise from a misinterpretation of these unpleasant, physical, fear-induced symptoms. Removal from the claustrophobic situation into open space leads to an immediate disappearance of fear.

Also, it is interesting to note that although claustrophobics commonly experience similar physical symptoms to other phobia victims, the feared outcomes or cognitive factors connected with these have a somewhat different emphasis. Suffocating, losing consciousness, exhausting the air supply and panic are all ahead of losing physical and mental control in a list of claustrophobic fears, whereas, in agoraphobia the latter is much more significant.

Similarly, and again in contrast with some other phobias, it is unusual for claustrophobics to misinterpret symptoms of chest pain or tightness, choking and breathlessness as signs of a heart attack. Almost invariably, these symptoms are believed to be connected with the threat of impending suffocation.

Suffocation by smothering
The third way in which suffocation can occur in real life is if breathing is physically impeded by smothering. However, it is thought that this is unlikely to contribute greatly to the fear in claustrophobia. Instead, the first and second aspects of suffocation (along with physical entrapment) are

felt by most experts to be the critical factors. These appear to be interrelated in that a claustrophobic person may misread fear symptoms (breathlessness, dizziness and so on) as signs of suffocation which, to him, indicates that the air supply is running out. Further evidence to support this view is suggested by the following two factors.

Firstly, it has been established that merely telling a claustrophobic person, however convincingly, about the facts concerning the provision of air in small spaces, how much is needed to survive and for how long, is largely ineffective in reducing fear. He may try to believe it but his own experience of supposed symptoms of suffocation is so strong that it convinces him otherwise. This is entirely consistent with the known, entrenched nature of phobic beliefs.

Secondly, the fear of a claustrophobic person in a small room usually increases if other people enter the space and this is because they are seen as competitors for the supposedly dwindling supply of air.

The other primary factor in claustrophobia, fear of physical restriction and entrapment, is believed to be correlated with suffocation anxiety in many cases. The two fears go hand-in-hand for most claustrophobics, and being physically restricted is also an unpleasant, or even traumatic experience, in unaffected people and in animals. It has been suggested that the connection with suffocation is that, in order to try to remove oneself from a situation in which the air supply is felt to be dwindling, one needs to be physically free.

The fear and feelings of inherent danger are thought to be the same whether one is physically immobilised by being, for example, tied up or wedged between rocks, or if free in body but unable to escape from a small space. Both involve entrapment and evidence, for example, from road or rail accidents shows that the overwhelming need experienced by survivors is to escape into open space and fresh air, away from danger.

Of course, many of the circumstances in which people become physically trapped are actually dangerous. Even when this is not the case, the situation may be threatening if a person can neither free himself nor realistically expect to be rescued, as he then faces the risk of death from hunger, thirst or exposure.

A knowledge of such dangers seems to be inherent in people from an early age and it is perhaps not surprising that a fear of them can contribute to claustrophobia.

Finally, in a minority of claustrophobics, the fear of entrapment appears to be the primary factor. These people do not report suffocation anxiety but still experience a claustrophobic response in any situation in which they feel that their bodily freedom is compromised.

Development of claustrophobia

Claustrophobia has provided fertile soil for those who believe that phobias can primarily be explained as an evolutionary or adaptive throwback to an earlier stage in human development – the preparedness theory (*see* Chapter 21).

It has also been suggested that human beings may possess an unconscious physiological, early-warning suffocation monitor that can detect interruptions in the air supply. It is postulated that a misfiring of this monitor may lead to the triggering of the suffocation alarm symptoms of claustrophobia but further research is needed to establish the validity of this theory.

Several researchers have examined the pathways leading to the acquisition of claustrophobia in individual people. Results indicate that a fairly high proportion can remember a direct, adverse, conditioning experience and one such event is sufficient to trigger claustrophobia. Also, surveys reveal that if the adverse experience contained the dual elements of entrapment and perceived threat to air supply then it is even more likely to lead to claustrophobia.

As mentioned above, generalised fears and beliefs about entrapment and suffocation are widespread. It is likely that indirect, vicarious conditioning along with disturbing information and accounts of claustrophobic experiences could lead to the development of the condition in susceptible people.

Treatment of claustrophobia

Four main methods of treatment have been applied to claustrophobia and these are graduated exposure, cognitive therapy, interoceptive therapy and single-session treatment based on intensive graduated exposure and discussion (*see* Chapter 22). Single-session treatment and exposure therapy have proved to be the most effective, followed by the cognitive and interoceptive approaches, with most patients showing reductions in fear and negative beliefs.

Patients whose pre-treatment beliefs in suffocation, entrapment and panic are high usually find that these are positively modified as a result of therapy. This is accompanied by a parallel decline in fear and in some people, negative beliefs are banished altogether and their claustrophobia is, in effect, cured. About eighty per cent of those who undergo therapy are greatly helped and find that claustrophobia no longer significantly impairs normal life.

The high success rate of therapy is particularly encouraging, given the entrenched nature of pre-treatment, negative cognitions in claustrophobia, which are not amenable to change by discussion alone. In common with other phobias, treatment allows the claustrophobic person to discover that his catastrophic cognitions do not come to pass. It is possible that including breathing or relaxation exercises and self-help measures in a treatment programme might also be of benefit, particularly to those who retain a reduced level of claustrophobia following therapy.

Chapter 14
Situational Specific Phobia:
Flying or Flight Phobia

Flight phobia is a fairly common condition that may affect as many as ten per cent of the population, with others reporting a lower level of anxiety and avoidance of flying whenever possible. It is evident that in the modern world of today, inability to cope with flying is a major disadvantage, especially for those whose work demands a great deal of travelling. On an everyday level, sufferers of flight phobia miss out on the opportunities for travel and holidays that, in the Western world at least, people now take for granted.

Symptoms of flight phobia

Flight phobia can accompany both claustrophobia and agoraphobia or exist entirely as a separate specific condition. Surveys have shown that more women than men are affected, with about seventy per cent of sufferers being female, and that the condition typically develops in young adulthood during the late twenties. Studies that have compared primary agoraphobics with secondary flight phobia to purely specific flight phobics have revealed some interesting differences concerning the nature and focus of the fear involved. Over seventy per cent of specific flight phobics were primarily fearful of the possibility of an air crash.

Development of flight phobia

The same seventy per cent of specific flight phobics have also stated that hearing and seeing news reports of air accidents figured prominently in the development of their phobia. This would appear to indicate that indirect, informational conditioning is important in the development of the condition. This was in marked contrast to a figure of eighteen per cent for agoraphobics. Also, about forty per cent of the specific flight phobic group had experienced one or more events that had frightened them during flying (such as turbulence) and pointed to these as the reasons behind the development of their condition.

Hence it would seem that in these people, such episodes acted as direct conditioning experiences. Some of the agoraphobics had also experienced turbulence or other types of eventful flight but did not regard them as significant. For the agoraphobic group, the fear of having a panic attack or losing control during a flight, was the main focus for their fear and the primary reason why they avoided air travel.

Among those in both groups who had actually experienced an in-flight panic attack, equal numbers believed that this was significant in the development of their phobia. However, agoraphobics believed that if the threat of a panic attack was removed they would no longer avoid flying. In contrast, specific flight phobics believed that the absence of panic symptoms would not materially alter their fear of flying. Also, among those in this group who had witnessed someone else becoming fearful during a flight, a fairly small but significant number believed that this had affected either the development or the maintenance of their own phobia. This points again to the role of vicarious, indirect conditioning experiences in the development of flight phobia.

Treatment of flight phobia

Studies indicate that graduated exposure, along with discussion and challenges to the negative cognitions attached to flying, is probably the most useful treatment for flight phobia. In practice, however, this is difficult to implement with the result that many therapists resort to indirect methods such as systematic desensitisation employing the person's imagination (that is, recreating in the mind the feared experiences of flying) and, possibly, film or video material. Also, the therapist will often instruct the person in relaxation techniques and methods of coping with his feared cognitions, or attempt to alter these by discussion.

At the end of the period of treatment, the person is encouraged to undertake a test flight and to report back to the therapist. It is usually found that the experience of undertaking the test flight, thereby challenging negative beliefs, is extremely effective in reducing fear. Therapy helps to reduce the general anxiety connected with the phobia and arms the person with coping strategies so that he is much more likely to undertake a test flight. Following the treatment and test flight, the person is generally able to undertake further journeys by air which again diminishes phobic fear.

In Sweden, thanks to the help and cooperation of Scandinavian Airlines, it became possible to carry out a single-session exposure treatment study on one group of flight-phobic patients (Öst, Brandberg and Alm, 1997). Free tickets were issued for internal, domestic return flights from and to Stockholm and the whole experience of taking the airport bus, checking in, obtaining a seat number and boarding pass and flying were used in treatment. Each patient was accompanied by a therapist with discussion concerning his beliefs, fears and feelings challenged at every stage.

Having made the outward flight and disembarked, therapist and patient were required to almost immediately re-engage in the process of boarding for their return, with each flight lasting about one hour. Hence total flying time was two hours with additional time added on at the airport and using the airport bus. The great majority of patients who underwent the treatment were able to fly unaccompanied afterwards and in most cases this improvement continued without relapse.

Chapter 15
Situational Specific Phobia:
Accident Phobia

Accident phobia has been studied most extensively in relation to accidents involving motor vehicles. It has been established that thirty-eight per cent of survivors of car crashes subsequently develop severe phobic fear and avoidance of car travel, which has had a significant effect on their normal life.

Symptoms of accident phobia

Although it is unusual for car journeys to be avoided completely, accident phobics will often only travel when strictly necessary. Also, the journey may only be undertaken at a particular time of day, for example, when traffic conditions are light. Accident phobics experience considerable anticipatory anxiety before the journey and are highly fearful while in the car. Some find it very difficult to be passengers and most constantly give the driver instructions.

It is not unusual for accident phobics to make considerable adjustments to their life to avoid car travel. This can include such extreme measures as moving house or even relinquishing a job and, in most cases, the person's normal enjoyment of outings, hobbies, holidays and so on, is considerably restricted because of the effect on mobility. It is possible that similar levels of phobic fear and avoidance may occur in those who have been in accidents involving buses, coaches and trains.

Development of accident phobia

Accident phobia is atypical in that it is closely linked with post-traumatic stress disorder (see page 41) but has, as its main elements, phobic fear and avoidance. There may be some difficulty in distinguishing between the two conditions, both of which have a motor vehicle accident as their primary causative factor. This is also unusual, since in most specific phobias, a traumatic event (conditioning factor) does not account for all cases.

The recently developed Accident Fear Questionnaire of American Psychiatry appears to reliably differentiate between the two conditions and indicates that phobic fear develops independently of injury, pain or depression caused by the accident. There is, however, some evidence that a person's psychological make-up might predispose them towards developing accident phobia (*see* below).

It is a central premise in the identification of phobia that the fear involved should be excessive and unreasonable and out of proportion to the situation. This could be regarded in two ways in accident phobia for, on the one hand, excessive fear of road travel when one has already survived a traumatic accident does not seem to be unreasonable. However, non-phobics who have suffered similar accidents do not become extremely anxious and are able to resume car travel. They may experience some initial anxiety but it is at a level that can be safely coped with and it tends to subside as time passes and driving resumes its former place in everyday life.

One study showed that over forty per cent of phobics expected to be involved in another accident in the near future, if they resumed travelling by car, whereas non-phobics had no such expectation. A higher proportion of phobics, compared to non-phobics, have a past history of anxiety prior to their motor vehicle accident. It is possible that psychological factors confer a greater risk of developing accident phobia and, once in place, the phobic has a propensity to regard himself as a victim rather than a survivor.

Treatment of accident phobia

Treatment for accident phobia is in a process of continual development and refinement. Initial cognitive therapy is needed, aimed at helping the person to realise that he is a survivor, and that there is no reason to suppose that an accident that has happened once will be repeated. Therapy using the person's imagination, and the use of video-taped material may be useful. Eventually, the person is encouraged to embark upon exposure therapy by becoming a car passenger – something that most phobics find extremely difficult. The final stage, if the person is a driver, is for him to start driving again and a refresher instruction course may help in this respect.

Chapter 16
Specific Phobia, Others
Subgroup: Water Phobia

The others subgroup includes all specific phobias which cannot readily be assigned to any of the other four subgroups. As such, it is not possible to identify any meaningful general characteristics but a glance at the phobias list confirms that the phobic stimuli for the others subgroup is extremely diverse. Also, while some of the phobias in the group are rare, others are apparently fairly common. Examples of both are included here and in the next four chapters.

On first consideration, water phobias could perhaps be more accurately assigned to the natural environment subgroup and this is a simple matter when the phobic stimuli are rivers, lakes, the ocean or waterfalls. However, a closer look at the nature of water phobia reveals a somewhat different picture which justifies its inclusion in the others subgroup.

Symptoms of water phobia in children

The condition is prevalent in young children in whom it typically appears before the age of five years and it manifests itself as an intense fear of bathing. This may later extend to any circumstance in which the child is expected to enter water (for example, paddling in streams or at the seaside). Most parents of water phobic children cannot remember a time when their child did not scream upon being bathed. It is not unusual for a newborn baby to cry when bathed for the first time. However, more often than not, babies soon not only become accustomed to the bath but obviously enjoy the whole experience. The phobic baby continues to cry each time he is placed in the water.

As the child grows older and more able to give voice to his fears, he may plead for hours not to be bathed and turn bathtime into a battleground. In the most severely affected children, parents may have to resort to cutting hair very short and giving sponge baths and it is these families who usually appear at clinics seeking help.

Studies suggest that for most small children, fears about bathing subside through repeated experience, although anxiety about, or dislike of, hair-washing and water going on the face may persist for a longer time. For slightly older children, water fear more commonly becomes associated with acquiring swimming skills. It is very common for children to fear ducking their head beneath the water and this can inhibit learning to swim and enjoyment of swimming activities. For water phobic children, however, even entering the swimming pool is impossible.

Evidence suggests that between two and a half and

five per cent of children aged up to twelve years are water phobic and that the condition is equally prevalent in boys and girls. One study showed that water phobia in children was in third place in a list of eighty phobias only surpassed by fear of snakes and rats. The fact that water phobia is clearly focussed on bathing and entering the water, rather than on water in the natural environment as such, is the reason why it is appropriate to place it in the others subgroup.

Symptoms of water phobia in adults

Figures for the incidence of water phobia in adults are not available but adults do not commonly come forward for treatment. This is the case for very many phobias and it can be safely suggested that there may be a higher number of sufferers than is indicated by available data.

However, the picture that emerges in adults appears to be somewhat different from that for children. Although fear of bathing is not unknown in adults, the main focus of fear appears to be on drowning and on being submerged. This is frequently connected with irrational cognitions surrounding water, such as fear of being suddenly engulfed by the sea, while sitting on the beach, or fear that a fish tank full of water will shatter and drown the person.

Hence, phobic adults may be extremely fearful of going anywhere near natural bodies of water. They cannot enjoy walking on a beach or travel on boats or ships and have never been able to learn to swim. The frequency of these types of fears may, in fact, be quite high. It is possible that readers have encountered at least one person who admits to fear or hatred of water to the extent that he or she has never been able to learn to swim.

Development of water phobia

Very few studies have been carried out on the nature of the development of water phobia in adults. However, it is likely that many of them have carried an early childhood fear of bathing into adult life, probably with some alteration in the focus of the phobia. In others, the onset of water phobia may be entirely different – at present, no study data is available, perhaps reflecting the general scarcity of adult subjects.

On the basis of the few studies that have been published, some interesting facts concerning the origins of water phobia in children have begun to emerge. When parents were questioned, the majority believed that their child had always been phobic from the very first time of being bathed in infancy. A further quarter were able to point to indirect conditioning events as having influenced the development of the phobia but only two per cent reported a direct, traumatic experience.

This is in marked contrast to some other specific phobias, in which direct, traumatic encounters with the feared stimulus appear to have a greater influence on development.

Indirect or vicarious conditioning, reported by about one quarter of those surveyed, was sometimes connected to the child observing other family members who were afraid of water. It is possible that this indicates some genetic, familial predisposition to water phobia but more probable that if a parent, particularly the mother with whom young children usually spend most of their time, is water fearful, her fear will be communicated to her offspring.

The present state of knowledge has led to a number of theories being put forward to explain the origins of water phobia. It has been suggested that an innate fear of water is present in young children but that it usually diminishes and disappears with repeated, non-fearful experience (*see* habituation, page 229) and normal development. The fear may be more highly developed in some individuals, possibly due to genetic factors. Those who become water phobic may have less opportunity to experience habituation because of their fear.

Family circumstances may be influential. One survey showed that adult water phobics frequently had little or no childhood experience of swimming, the seaside or water-related activities because these were not regarded as important in their family. Water phobia may lend itself to an evolutionary explanation for its development.

Treatment of water phobia

As mentioned above, very few water phobic adults seek help for their condition, hence treatment has almost entirely been aimed at children. The most effective treatment for children appears to be a combination of modelling and graduated, *in vivo* exposure to water.

One study compared three different treatments with a control group. A number of highly fearful children of both sexes, aged between three and eight years, were arbitrarily placed in one of four groups.

Group One watched a therapist model gradually more difficult activities at the swimming pool, which eventually involved entering, and performing tasks in, the water. Each child was then asked to undertake the same series of tasks, encouraged, aided (when necessary) and praised by the therapist but with no further modelling.

Group Two watched the therapist model a series of sports activities in a games room next to the swimming pool. They were then each asked to perform the identical series of water activities undertaken by the first group, in the same way.

Group Three watched the therapist model the water-related activities. Each was then asked to participate with the therapist in the sports activities that had been modelled for the second group.

Group Four were controls who received no treatment.

Groups One and Two both made similar progress as a result of treatment. However, three months later, Group One had retained and improved on their position whereas Group Two had lost some of their early gains and once again become more fearful. Group Three showed no change in their fear of water following treatment.

It is possible to devise a similar treatment plan for young children with bathing phobia, based on modelling and graduated exposure, which is effective. Studies also indicate that a reduction of fear in one aspect of water phobia, such as bathing, significantly reduces anxiety in other situations, for example, going to the beach. It is hoped that more research into, and understanding of, the mechanisms underlying water phobia will enable further refinements in treatment programmes to be made, particularly with regard to adult sufferers.

Chapter 17
Specific Phobia, Others
Subgroup: Acrophobia

Acrophobia or height phobia is a common specific phobia which may affect as many as five per cent of the population at any one time. The condition afflicts both males and females and a wide range of acrophobic stimuli can elicit a fearful response, such as high-rise buildings, cliff tops, bridges, upper decks of a ship, flights of stairs, escalators, lifts, ladders and air travel.

Symptoms of acrophobia (height phobia)

It is common for acrophobics to be fearful of, and to avoid, all types of high places. Also, phobic fear may be experienced in relation to heights which non-affected people would consider to be quite modest. In common with many other phobias, height phobics generally try to cope by avoidance of all high places.

However, while this may once have been possible, it is no longer so in most modern cities of the world. High-rise offices, stores and apartments are a fact of life for most people, necessitating the use of long flights of stairs, lifts or escalators. Road and rail travel frequently involve passing over bridges and flyovers. In such environments, it can be appreciated that being acrophobic can have a severe effect upon a person's way of life.

Development of acrophobia

Recent studies have revealed some interesting aspects of height phobia although, as with most phobias, questions remain to be answered. The condition has apparently been present in human beings for a very long time and is mentioned in early historical writings, for example, those of Hippocrates. A well-developed sense of caution in relation to high places would seem to be a sensible (survival) attribute for human beings, who are the least agile of the primates. This has led several researchers to believe that biological or evolutionary factors have an impact upon the acquisition of height phobia (*see* Chapter 21).

A fascinating series of experiments carried out in the 1960s showed that fear of heights is present once a baby is able to move around independently. The experiments involved the use of a piece of apparatus called the 'visual cliff'. This was a large, strong sheet of glass, which was supported at a height above the floor and across the centre of which was placed a wooden board. On one half, a patterned paper was stuck to the underside of the glass so that the floor could not be seen and the surface appeared solid. On the other half, the patterned material was placed on the floor below the glass. So, although the glass provided a solid surface, because it presented no visual barrier, there was an apparent drop to the floor.

Babies who were able to crawl were tested on the visual cliff. Each was placed on the centre board and the child's mother would then call to the baby from either side of the apparatus. While the babies would quite readily crawl onto the 'no drop' half of the glass with the patterned paper, they would not venture onto the 'cliff side' even though they were able to feel that the glass was solid. The same results were obtained with other young animals – lambs, kids and chicks.

Later experiments proved that the fear response (measured as a rise in heartbeat rate) only occurred if the baby had learnt to crawl. Younger babies who were not yet able to move independently, showed no change in heartbeat rate if they were placed on the 'cliff' side of the glass.

These results, along with other research, have led some experts to formulate the non-associative theory (*see* page 220) for the acquisition of this and certain other specific phobias such as water phobia (*see* page 187). Essentially, the argument is that the phobia in later life is produced from an innate, developmental fear which does not require any adverse or other conditioning event to come into being. The theory may be supported by evidence that has been obtained from directly questioning, and assessing, acrophobics who have sought treatment. This has shown that only about twelve per cent of acrophobics recall direct, adverse experiences connected with heights, relevant to the onset of their condition.

Most believe that their phobia has always been present and can apparently be accounted for by non-associative theory. Adherents to the theory suggest that in most people, additional experience gained during maturation leads to a decline in fear of heights to a level that might be termed 'normal caution' (habituation). However, in those who become phobic, this process, for some reason, does not take place and fear, at this stage, may then be influenced by other factors. Not all experts subscribe to the theory but evidence does at least seem to suggest that the early, developmental fear of heights in children may be relevant.

A further interesting aspect of height phobia is that surveys reveal that acrophobics do not necessarily realise that their fear is unreasonable. Hence, they lack the insight (which is set out as one of the diagnostic criteria for specific phobia) that their fear is excessive and out of proportion to the situation. One study compared the beliefs and fear levels of a group of acrophobics and a non-phobic control group in relation to ascending a three-tier, extendable ladder.

Before the test, the acrophobic group experienced much higher levels of anticipatory anxiety and most believed that they would fall and sustain severe injuries. Also, they held to the view that their anxiety was not inappropriate, in view of the fact that they were going to be asked to climb the ladder. The control group lacked anticipatory anxiety and had low expectations of danger in relation to the ladder test. Similar results have been obtained using fear questionnaires for acrophobia and it has further been revealed that people with this condition have low levels of belief in their ability to cope.

Treatment of acrophobia (height phobia)

Various experts have conducted trials of different forms of treatment for acrophobia based on behavioural therapy, cognitive therapy and cognitive–behavioural therapy. *In vivo* exposure-based treatments, conducted with the aid of a therapist, are the most successful and particularly encouraging results have been obtained from a technique known as guided mastery. However, it is felt by some experts that further attention should be directed towards the range of negative cognitions attached to acrophobia. Attempting to alter these beliefs prior to an exposure-based treatment programme might prove to be helpful.

Chapter 18
Specific Phobia, Others
Subgroup: Choking Phobia

Symptoms of choking phobia

Choking phobia is an apparently rare condition characterised by an excessive fear of choking to death on food, drink, medicines or tablets. It is more usually associated with food or pills rather than with fluids and sufferers typically have difficulty with eating. They tend to eat items that they regard as safer foods such as soup, purées, yoghurt, etc, but even these are avoided as much as possible so that sufferers usually lose weight. Food is chewed excessively before it is swallowed to further reduce the perceived risk of choking.

Victims recognise that their fear is excessive and would like to be able to eat normally and hence are clearly distinguishable from people suffering from anorexia nervosa or other eating disorders.

They can also be readily distinguished from people suffering from 'globus' which is defined as a feeling of having a lump in one's throat when swallowing. This condition was originally called *Globus Hystericus* as it was formerly believed to typically be a symptom of acute anxiety.

However, doctors now recognise that the sensation of globus can have a physical cause such as the throat having been previously scratched by a hard piece of food. Whatever the cause, people with globus report discomfort upon swallowing and are not afraid of choking. Difficulty in swallowing connected with a definite physical disorder (commonly of the oesophagus) is called dysphagia. Hence, choking phobia can be easily distinguished from this condition which has an identifiable organic cause.

Development of choking phobia

The current state of knowledge suggests that this phobia typically arises suddenly after a person has suffered a frightening and traumatic choking episode. Once again, the unreasonableness of phobic fear arising out of such an experience could be open to question.

Most readers will have experienced a mild attack of choking and will know just how unpleasant this can be. Others may perhaps have been 'winded' and can remember the frightening sensation of being momentarily unable to draw breath.

It is evident that choking is extremely distressing and frightening. Also, although it is uncommon, people do sometimes die as a result of choking on a piece of food or other material which they are unable to dislodge by the normal means of coughing. Sometimes, a person only survives because someone else has been on hand to help, perhaps by performing Heimlich's manoeuvre. Hearing about choking incidents in others may contribute towards the maintenance of phobic fear, although it is thought to be less significant than the triggering, traumatic episode. Some choking phobics feel happier about eating when other people are present, as they know that they would receive the necessary help in an emergency.

One study has suggested that choking phobics are excessively concerned and anxious not only about the physical sensations connected with eating (chewing and swallowing, etc), but also about those produced by other bodily functions. It may be that these anxieties have always been present but are exacerbated by a choking episode and then contribute to the development of phobic fear. Alternatively, the heightened anxiety may itself result from the development of the phobia.

Another study suggested that people who are excessively frightened of death may be more at risk of developing the phobia following a choking experience. Given the significance of a triggering episode, it is perhaps not surprising that there is no particular age of onset for the phobia. Infants and people in older age are susceptible to choking episodes but these can also occur at any other time of life. Also, there appear to be no gender differences and choking phobia is equally likely to affect people of either sex.

Treatment of choking

Since choking phobia is relatively rare, no comparative studies have been carried out on treatment methods but successful outcomes have been reported using behavioural and cognitive–behavioural therapies and drugs. Behavioural therapy is based on graduated exposure which, in choking phobia, consists of encouraging the person to eat a series of foods beginning with 'safe,' soft items and then progressing to harder, more feared ones. This takes place with the aid of the therapist who also works with the patient to reduce chewing to normal levels.

Negative cognitions concerning eating and the risk of choking can be successfully reduced by these means in some people. In others, however, behavioural experiments may be helpful in challenging these such as ones designed to demonstrate the effectiveness of coughing and practising swallowing exercises. Some choking phobics have been helped by modern drug treatments and it is thought that selective serotonin re-uptake inhibitors (SSRIs) may prove useful. However, it is generally agreed that behavioural and cognitive–behavioural therapies offer the best treatment for all specific phobias, including choking phobia.

Chapter 19
Specific Phobia, Others
Subgroup: Dental Phobia

Symptoms of dental phobia

Anxiety and aversion connected with dental treatment is prevalent among children and adults alike, with phobia occurring at the extreme end of a scale of common human fears. Fear of dentistry appears to be prevalent in all countries where in-depth studies have been carried out. The method of assessment employed is usually some form of 'dental fears' questionnaire and results frequently show a high incidence of anxiety, which can be as great as thirty-six per cent, in those surveyed. The figures for true dental phobia vary somewhat between different surveys but appear to be within the range of three to five per cent for adults and six to seven per cent for children.

A far greater proportion, possibly as many as a third of adults, experience considerable anxiety, or dread visits to the dentist and avoid them as far as possible. Results indicate that dental phobia is more common in women than in men and that the most likely age group to be affected are older children and adolescents. The condition is less likely to appear for the first time in adult life and incidence decreases with age.

Research has shown that dental phobia is a complex condition in which many factors are at work. In common with other phobics, those suffering from dental phobia have a range of negative and/or catastrophic beliefs about dental procedures. These are not only concerned with aspects of treatment itself, such as expecting to experience painful injections, drilling, extractions, etc, or the belief that anaesthetic will not work, but also fear of panic, losing control or a dread that something terrible will happen. Phobics frequently harbour negative thoughts about dentists themselves, usually based on previous experiences. They may believe that dentists are unfeeling, cold and uncaring and likely to be impatient with adults who are fearful of treatment.

Another, perhaps surprising aspect, is the extent to which dental phobia apparently interferes with everyday life. One study revealed that half of dental phobics felt that their condition significantly impaired their social and family relationships. Typical fears concerned eating out and the need to keep teeth concealed, i.e. by covering the mouth with a hand when laughing, because the phobic believes that the state of his teeth would be noticed by others.

Also, personal relationships can be severely affected – the dental phobic may be reluctant to kiss or may come under pressure from family members to visit the dentist. Hence avoiding dental treatment does not ensure peace of mind for the phobic person. Indeed, evidence suggests that the dental phobic worries considerably about the state of his teeth and oral health and is disturbed by, for example, television adverts for toothpaste which depict tooth decay. Many are afraid to admit to, or discuss, their fears with others because they are afraid that they will be ridiculed. An adult dental phobic often believes that his fear is childish and something to be ashamed of.

There is some evidence to suggest that dental phobics experience elevated levels of anxiety in other aspects of life, perhaps due to their individual temperament. Temperamental differences might partly help to explain why, in a group of people who have seemingly had similar experiences of dental treatment, some are fearful while others are not. One study showed that a group of dental phobics who were successfully treated subsequently showed a significant reduction in the number of days taken off work and in their consumption of alcohol (previously used to ease general anxiety).

Development of dental phobia

A great deal of research has been directed towards attempting to discover the relevant factors in the development of dental phobia and several interesting aspects have emerged. As with other specific phobias, the role of adverse, and in this case, almost always painful, experiences of dental treatment have been examined. Adverse, 'conditioning' experiences evidently have a role to play and are reported by many dental phobics.

However, it appears that more than one painful episode may be necessary for the development of phobia. It is also the case that many non-phobics have had experience of painful dental treatment and so it seems that adverse experiences only provide a part of the answer. It may also be relevant that toleration of pain appears to differ between individuals with some people having a lower 'pain threshold' than others. It is possible that those with a lower toleration of pain may be more at risk of developing dental phobia.

It has been suggested that the experience of dental treatment is intrinsically adverse to human beings and hence fearfulness might be an expected result which could be explained as some kind of evolutionary, adaptive mechanism. (*See* Chapter 21.) Dental examination involves being tipped back to a supine position in a raised chair from which escape is difficult (the element of entrapment which is significant in claustrophobia).

Next, a person who is often only an acquaintance and sometimes a comparative stranger, places a number of instruments into the patient's mouth and has access to the vulnerable areas of the face and throat. It is possible to see that being in such a position would spell danger, and evoke fear, in ancient man. Proponents of evolutionary or preparedness theory suggest that some kind of 'memory' of this danger modified by the individual's own experiences could account for the development of dental phobic fear.

As mentioned above, the nature of the patient–dentist relationship in childhood is another relevant factor. Many of those who have had negative experiences with a dentist as children felt that this was a relevant factor in their present state of fear. They found it difficult to dispel the image of dentists as being uncaring and unsympathetic which reinforced their current fear and avoidance. The childhood relationship with the dentist seemed to be particularly significant in those who had *not* suffered pain during early treatments.

Interestingly, among a non-phobic control group who had experienced painful treatment during childhood, a majority felt that their dentist had been kind, caring and concerned. As might be expected, it would seem that the endurance of pain was made easier, and was less likely to have a lasting effect, if the dentist showed a kindly attitude.

Unfortunately, the significance of this information is hard to assess for two main reasons. Firstly, it relies upon the accuracy of an adult's past memories and secondly, it is possible for a highly anxious or uncooperative child to be completely mistaken about the attitude of the dentist.

Most dentists in modern practice go to great lengths to reassure children. Parents may be encouraged to bring along even very young children to their own check-up appointments so that their offspring can become accustomed to all the procedures at the dentist's surgery. It would be highly unusual today for any dentist to be unsympathetic towards a young patient and it will be interesting to see if this has a detectable impact on the future incidence of dental phobia.

Another factor that has been examined in relation to the development of dental phobia is the role of indirect, vicarious conditioning and information. It appears that parental anxiety, particularly on the part of the mother, concerning dental treatment is likely to influence children but that the children's own experience is the factor that confirms or disconfirms fear. Some experts have suggested that, rather than the fear being 'learnt' by the child's observation of a fearful parent, its existence represents a genetic predisposition for anxiety present in the family. As mentioned above, temperamental features, that may be governed by genetic rather than environmental influences, do seem to play a part in some cases of dental phobia. However, it may be that in any group of dental phobics, one or more interacting, causal factors may have been at work.

Once the phobia is established, there appear to be several reasons why it is maintained. Avoidance itself is one of these, but only partly for the usual reason in phobia that a lack of further experience of dental treatment does not allow disconfirmation of negative cognitions to take place. In fact, studies have shown that dental phobics and others who are highly fearful but who *do* continue to visit their dentist, often remain anxious. It seems that a lessening of fear very much depends upon the beliefs of the patient with regard to pain.

One study revealed that fear diminished with repeated dental treatment if two criteria were met. These were, firstly, if the actual experience of pain was less than that which had been anticipated and secondly, if the patient then believed that he could expect this pattern to continue. If a phobic person continued to expect high levels of pain, in spite of contradictory experience, his fear was more likely to be maintained. Repeated visits to the dentist for check-ups when no treatment is needed, also seems to be fairly ineffective in reducing fear. It has been suggested that the gap between such routine appointments is too long to play a useful part in behavioural exposure therapy.

A second aspect of avoidance in dental phobia is that it only brings about a temporary relief from anxiety. As mentioned above, avoiding the dentist increases anxiety in phobic people as they are often worried about the state of their teeth and are aware of the likely effects of neglect.

Treatment of dental phobia

Dental phobia appears to be a more complex condition than some of the other specific phobias due to the interaction of several different factors, of which the most important are experience and expectation of pain, the dentist–patient relationship, beliefs and ability to cope with anxiety. In view of this complexity, treatment methods have to be fairly broadly based and a variety of approaches have been tried.

Many of these are successful although it remains the case that a quarter to a third of patients are not helped by treatment. Both behavioural and cognitive–behavioural therapies have been tried. In some cases, these have incorporated relaxation techniques, methods of enhancing self-efficacy (the person's self-belief in his ability to cope with dental procedures) and control and communication strategies in which the patient is taught signals so that he can easily stop a procedure, or otherwise alert the dentist to any feelings of unease.

A group of patients who had received this type of treatment programme were questioned about its effectiveness. They revealed that being fully informed beforehand about their treatment, being able to believe that their dentist took their anxiety seriously and did not think them childish or silly, and being able to exercise a degree of control all helped to reduce fear and enabled them to cope with treatment. Hence it seems likely that for many dental phobics, the value of a good relationship with their dentist and their participation in therapy is of great importance.

Cognitive–behavioural therapies have been shown to help those with catastrophic beliefs concerning dental treatment and those in whom fear of panic attack is a prominent feature. It is hoped that further research into the nature of dental phobia will allow new treatment programmes to be developed and evaluated, particularly with a view to aiding those who are currently not being helped by treatment.

Chapter 20
Specific Phobia, Others
Subgroup: Taijin-Kyofu-Sho

Taijin-Kyofu-Sho or TKS is a very interesting and unusual phobia because it is almost entirely confined to the Japanese and appears to arise directly out of Japanese social behaviour.

TKS is a form of social phobia but with the crucial difference that the fear is of causing embarrassment or offence to *other* people by the way one behaves. Sufferers from TKS are typically afraid that they will cause this offence or embarrassment by, for example, staring at other people (particularly at their intimate areas), pulling faces, blushing or flatulence.

Japanese social interactions are governed by a code of behaviour that requires the individual to read subtle signs in others and to be highly attentive to their feelings and needs. One is expected to be able to do this without the need for spoken communication and to place the wishes of others before one's own.

Within this cultural framework, it is possible to make mistakes and inadvertently cause others to feel uncomfortable, although this is not usually a problem. A TKS sufferer is, however, excessively fearful of this happening and the anxiety is felt most acutely in the

212

company of acquaintances and work colleagues. He usually feels much less anxious with family and close friends and also with complete strangers.

TKS affects a greater number of men than women and it usually arises in the teenage years. It is rare for it to appear for the first time in middle age, but it is a commonly reported phobia in Japan and occasionally occurs in Japanese people living in other parts of the world.

Chapter 21
The Development of Phobias

In recent years, a considerable amount of research in clinical psychology has been devoted to attempting to explain why human beings should be afflicted by phobias. Psychologists have formulated various theoretical models for the development of phobias and have attempted to test the validity of their theories by conducting controlled experiments with phobic people in a clinical setting.

A second area of research involves evaluating the mechanisms that may be at work in maintaining phobias, once they are in place, and several of these have already been mentioned in previous chapters.

The aetiology or development of phobias is a complex subject and one in which there is considerable disagreement among experts, with some favouring one model over another. Others believe that no single model can account for all phobias and that there are several different, underlying, developmental mechanisms at work. Grouping phobias according to their aetiology might, in fact, produce a quite different set of categories to those that are currently in use.

A full understanding of the theoretical, developmental models of phobias requires considerable knowledge of psychology and is beyond the scope of this book. In the following discussion, an attempt is made to simplify and summarise some of the complex ideas that are involved.

One critical factor that psychologists have had to address is the reason why some fears are so much more common than others.

The non-random distribution of phobic fears

Although it is known that almost any stimulus can provoke a phobic response, some are evidently far more likely to do so, and this phenomenon is known as the 'non-random distribution of phobic fears'.

Any attempt to account for phobias has to try and explain why fear of spiders, snakes, heights, enclosed spaces, water, crowds, storms, blood, and social gatherings should be so much more prevalent than fear of, for example, cows, rocks or electricity.

Earlier studies of phobias assumed that they were *all* acquired at an unconscious level and were completely unaffected by individual beliefs, thoughts, emotions or assumptions. The latter, which have come to be known as 'cognitive factors', are now recognised to be enormously important in the maintenance of phobic fears and almost certainly contribute to their development as well.

In general, aetiological models of phobias fall into three broad categories, the first of which are those that are thought to operate mainly at the unconscious level, while the second are those that fall within reach of conscious thought. However, it is now accepted by many experts that there is probably a considerable degree of overlap between the two, and this provides the third category.

Some of the 'unconscious' models can further be considered to operate on the (human) species as a whole, as well as working at an individual level. These include some of those which fall under the broad umbrella of evolutionary ('biological') models.

Classical conditioning is an example of an unconscious, biological model working at individual level. While it has long been recognised that, standing alone, it cannot provide an adequate explanation for the development of phobias, the whole process of conditioning has been re-examined and refined in recent years.

Modern conditioning models take cognitive factors into account and hence recognise an interaction between unconscious and conscious psychological processes (the third category). These refined conditioning models are believed by some experts to be more than adequate to account for most cases of phobia. Other models concentrate mainly on the cognitive (conscious) factors involved in phobias and so are best grouped into the second category mentioned above.

Evolutionary models and theories (mainly belonging to the unconscious category)

The essence of Darwinian evolutionary theory is that slight changes in biological features, which are themselves determined by genes, can arise by chance in individuals of a species. If such a change gives an individual a slight advantage, it is likely to be successful in breeding and to pass the characteristic on to its offspring. Over a period of time, increasing numbers of individuals will come to possess the changed characteristic, as long as it continues to be advantageous and this is known as adaptation.

Some experts in psychology believe that similar evolutionary or adaptationist arguments can help to explain certain human behavioural and anxiety disorders, including phobias. Strictly speaking, in order for evolutionary or adaptationist theories to be credible, it would be necessary to demonstrate that behavioural disorders are genetically controlled. Psychologists who support the theories take as their starting point the widely accepted view that the generation of anxiety or fear in the appropriate circumstances (for example, danger), is of survival value to an individual and to a species. Fear, and the heightened state of physiological arousal and alertness that accompanies it, is present not only in human beings but in many animal species as well, and so it is easy to accept that its existence confers an adaptive advantage. Also, the physiological or biological processes that can be involved in fear, such as the release of the hormone adrenaline to prepare the body for 'fright, flight or fight', are undoubtedly under genetic control.

'Evolutionary' psychologists point to data that suggests that there is indeed a familial, and hence, possibly, a genetic tendency for at least some phobic fears. They also believe that the clustering of phobic fears around certain stimuli (i.e. the non-random distribution) itself invites an adaptationist explanation. They suggest that even though phobias are concerned with seemingly irrational fears, they can be, at least partly, accounted for by evolutionary models and theories. Two of the most important of these are described below.

Preparedness theory

Preparedness theory, which was first suggested about thirty years ago, rests on two assumptions. The first is that human beings possess a predisposition or 'preparedness' to fear certain stimuli. These stimuli would have once represented danger to early man and hence fear and physiological arousal in response to them conferred an advantage according to evolutionary principles.

Evolution works on an extremely long timescale but

mankind has advanced very rapidly. Hence the predisposition for certain fears persists in the human species, even though the stimuli themselves are no longer so relevant. However, preparedness on its own does not explain the existence of phobias.

The second assumption is that classical Pavlovian conditioning (*see* page 221), that is the occurrence of an unpleasant or traumatic experience (the unconditioned stimulus or UCS) in the presence of the stimulus, activates phobia. Therefore, according to preparedness theory, evolutionary processes from the past and conditioning processes acting on an individual in the present, produce phobia. Those who advocate the theory believe that it explains the non-random distribution of phobic fears. Indeed, some studies have shown that it is relatively easy to induce physiological 'fear' responses (measured by skin conductance tests and heartbeat rate) to stimuli that are commonly involved in phobias.

A further refinement of the theory has been the proposal that two types of adaptive fear system have been written into the human psyche by evolution. The first is called the 'predator defence system' which is the one believed to be activated in the case of animal or 'danger' phobias such as height phobia.

The second is the 'social-submissiveness system' which is believed to be tuned to stimuli that enabled early human beings to find their place in the hierarchy of their family or tribal group. Angry or disapproving faces or threatening gestures are the type of stimuli that are thought likely to have been involved. It is suggested that it is this social-submissiveness system which is somehow triggered by an adverse conditioning experience in cases of social phobia.

While there is some evidence to support certain aspects of preparedness theory including a number of results from laboratory studies (*see* pre-attentive mechanisms, page 223) it is not universally accepted. One of the main problems is the overwhelming evidence for the part played by cognitive factors in phobia which is not allowed for within the preparedness concept.

Non-associative theory

Non-associative theory has similarities to the preparedness model outlined above, but is more restricted in that it is aimed at accounting for specific phobias and developmental fears that arise in childhood.

It is suggested that most of the stimuli that elicit specific phobias are ones that represented danger to early human beings, particularly to young children if they wandered away from their parents. Heightened anxiety, physiological arousal and awareness of danger increased the likelihood of survival and so innate fear responses in the presence of such prepotent stimuli were adaptive and became incorporated into the make-up of human beings.

Non-associative theory proposes that the innate fear response is likely to be activated in a young child on his or her very first encounter with a prepotent stimulus, *without* the need for any traumatic or adverse experience. It is suggested that, in the normal course of events, individual experience causes fear to diminish and eventually disappear, i.e. habituation takes place. However, in a few children, this process does not occur and fear remains strong, resulting in phobia. The phobia may be carried into adult life but if it arises later, it may represent a reactivation of an innate developmental fear. It is suggested that this might even be triggered by some unrelated stressful experience such as bereavement or depression.

While non-associative theory provides some useful arguments, it is generally felt that it is inadequate to explain specific phobias but may be able to account for some of the developmental fears of childhood. One of the main objections is that there is a great deal of evidence to suggest that traumatic (conditioning) experiences play an important part in many cases of specific phobia and this is not allowed for within non-associative theory.

Other unconscious models and mechanisms

Classical (Pavlovian) conditioning

Classical conditioning is based on the experimental work of the Russian physiologist, Ivan Pavlov, who, in the early 1900s, demonstrated that dogs can be 'conditioned' to associate one stimulus with a second, unrelated one. Pavlov gave the dogs a small amount of meat causing them to salivate, which was a normal, unconditioned response (UCR) to the presence of food while at the same time setting off a metronome or ringing a bell or buzzer. After a few repeated trials, the dogs salivated in anticipation of receiving food merely upon hearing the clicking of the metronome or the sound of the bell when no meat was given to them.

The food in these experiments was the conditioned stimulus (CS) while the metronome or bell was the unconditioned stimulus (UCS), with salivation becoming the conditioned response (CR) or conditioned reflex.

Similar conditioning experiments have been carried out with many other animals, establishing that it readily takes place and produces an automatic (i.e. non-cognitive) response. By 1920, an attempt had been made to establish that conditioning also occurs in humans, on the basis of an experiment that was carried out with an eleven-month-old baby boy called Albert (Watson and Rayner, 1920).

'Little Albert' had a pet white rat with which he liked to play. In the experiment every time he approached the rat (the CS) an iron bar was struck, making a loud and frightening noise, close beside him (the UCS). The child was frightened by the noise (the UCR) and after five similar exposures, became fearful at the sight of the rat (CR) without the bar being struck. On the basis of these experiments, it was suggested that conditioning could account for most cases of phobia, but the theory soon ran in to problems which still hold true today. Briefly, these objections are:

1. Within the same phobia, some sufferers have had traumatic experiences while others have not, so the significance of conditioning appears to vary.
2. Not all people who have traumatic experiences go on to develop phobia.
3. Classical conditioning theory would suggest that any repeated pairing of a CS and a traumatic UCS should produce a phobic response to the CS, in which case unusual phobias could be expected to be more common. However, in fact, there is a definite bias and ease of acquiring phobias to certain types of stimuli which argues against simple classical conditioning.
4. Vicarious conditioning, informational, emotional and cognitive factors have all been shown to be important in both the acquisition and maintenance of phobias. Once again, these are not allowed for in classical conditioning.

Pre-attentive mechanisms

Supporters of pre-attentive theory take as their initial hypothesis, the proposal that phobic fear to stimuli which, in an evolutionary context, posed a threat to the survival of early human beings, is activated at an unconscious level.

They argue that a rapid, unconscious activation of fear and alertness to a dangerous stimulus conferred a survival advantage and so became incorporated into the make-up of human beings.

A series of experiments were carried out (using skin conductance responses measured electrically as an indication of fear) upon specific phobics and non-phobic controls. The phobic subjects were fearful of either snakes or spiders. All the subjects were shown a series of slides, depicting snakes, spiders, flowers and mushrooms. However, some of the pictures were disguised (masked) and unrecognisable because they had been cut up, reassembled at random and re-photographed. It was discovered that phobic people showed measurably increased fear in response to both masked and unmasked slides of their particular phobic stimulus, supporting the theory of the existence of pre-attentive mechanisms.

Leading on from these discoveries, it has been suggested that classical conditioning acting upon unconscious pre-attentive mechanisms is responsible for cases of animal phobia and, possibly for social phobia as well. A complicated series of experiments seemed to demonstrate that people could be conditioned to fear relevant phobic stimuli at an unconscious level. It is suggested that once in place, the fear may be worked upon by conscious, cognitive processes but that these are important for the maintenance of phobia rather than for its initiation. Once again, although there appears to be a great deal of interesting experimental evidence to support the theory, it is not universally accepted by all experts. The main objection is that thoughts and beliefs available to the conscious mind are felt by many to be critical, not only in the continuance of phobias but in their development as well.

Cognitive models for the development and maintenance of phobias (conscious category)

Cognitive models for the development and maintenance of phobias are built around the misconceptions held not only by phobic people themselves, but by anxious individuals in general. It has been established that phobic people mistakenly believe that the feared subject or situation is highly dangerous for them. They experience high levels of anticipatory anxiety and are afraid of catastrophic consequences if they are forced to confront the feared subject. The catastrophic consequences may concern the stimulus itself such as the probability of attack by an animal in the case of animal phobia or being humiliated in public in social phobia.

Also, however, the phobic person fears catastrophic consequences that are attached to himself such as his own inability to cope, the likelihood of a panic attack, mental and physical collapse or heart attack. Studies have shown that, in advance of a confrontation with something that they are afraid of, most people tend to overestimate the degree of fear that they will actually experience. Phobic people are particularly likely to do this and the tendency has become known as 'the over-prediction of fear'. Some cognitive models propose that the origins of phobias lie, at least, partly, within the realm of the inaccurately predicted fears and misconceptions held by vulnerable people. Such people may, for some reason, be particularly at risk of phobia development in certain circumstances because of the existence of their negative cognitions.

A considerable amount of evidence has been gathered (some of which has been described in the preceding text) which demonstrates the importance of cognitive factors in various aspects of phobia. One particularly important factor appears to be the way in which negative beliefs can be changed completely by successful phobia treatments. It is thought that ongoing research will continue to shed light on this complex and interesting aspect of phobia.

Conscious or unconscious models of phobia

Some experts feel that a combination of conscious and unconscious processes, possibly with differing degrees of significance between the various phobias, can most usefully explain phobic responding. Models that come into this category may well incorporate a modern view of conditioning, which allows for the impact of existing beliefs, past and present experiences, vicarious learning and information and emotional factors. The theoretical concepts behind such models are complex and beyond the scope of this book but they offer a useful contribution towards an understanding of the development and maintenance of phobias.

Chapter 22
The Treatment of Phobias

Some of the various therapies and treatments for phobias have already been referred to in preceding chapters. The aim of this section is to define the terminology used by psychologists involved in treating phobias and to briefly describe the various therapies. Pharmacological treatments for phobias are also discussed, while 'alternative therapies', which may be helpful for some phobics, are listed and described in Chapter 24. Psychological therapies fall broadly into the two categories of behavioural and cognitive but, in practice, a treatment programme may contain elements of both.

Behavioural therapies

Before describing the therapies themselves, it may be helpful to define two processes (extinction and habituation) that are commonly referred to by behavioural psychologists. These processes may take place as a result of treatment but can also, to a certain extent, occur naturally.

Extinction is a progressive weakening and eventual disappearance of the conditioned, fearful response as a result of non-traumatic exposures or experiences with the feared (phobic) stimulus. Hence a new non-fearful coupling between the stimulus and response is generated which is mediated by learning.

Habituation, in essence, means 'getting used to'. In psychology, it refers to the decline in the conditioned, fearful response which occurs with repeated exposure to the feared (phobic) stimulus. Eventually, the fearful, conditioned response may disappear completely. In practical terms and to non-psychologists, there would appear to be very little difference between extinction and habituation!

Different forms of exposure to a feared stimulus

All behavioural therapies for phobia involve various forms of exposure to the feared stimulus. The methods used vary and may be afforded differing degrees of importance, depending upon the views and approach of individual clinicians.

Imaginal exposure
A form of unreal exposure in which the sufferer is asked to imagine encounters with the phobic subject. The imagined situations are manipulated in various ways by the therapist in order to help reduce fear. Imaginal exposure may be used in conjunction with real, in vivo exposure (*see* page 230).

Exposure using photographs, videos or computer graphics ('virtual' exposure)
As the title implies, a form of unreal exposure using modern media.

In vivo exposure

This refers to actual, real-life exposure to the phobic stimulus and can be used in a variety of different ways, as listed below:

1. *Flooding or intense exposure* Sudden intense and prolonged exposure (over a number of hours or longer) to the feared stimulus. Although it can be effective, especially with children, flooding is a type of treatment that is feared by phobic people and one to which they are unlikely to give prior consent.
2. *Graded exposure* Exposure to the feared stimulus which gradually increases in intensity over the period of treatment.
3. *Massed exposure* A treatment programme that involves exposure to the feared stimulus on a daily basis.
4. *Spaced exposure* A treatment programme that involves exposure to the feared stimulus on a weekly basis for a fairly prolonged period.
5. *Therapist-directed exposure* which may include all of the above.
6. *Self-directed exposure* A treatment programme (that may have been initially suggested by a therapist) which the patient undertakes himself.

Systematic desensitisation

A form of behavioural therapy that has been particularly successful in treating phobic children. It involves working out a 'fear hierarchy' with each child (i.e. least to most feared situation) and training the patient in relaxation skills which are then employed in a series of imaginal, graded exposure trials. The relaxation skills, which are successfully mastered and practised in advance by the patient, inhibit and combat the anxiety response.

Emotive imagery

An adaptation of systematic desensitisation which is sometimes used with children. A fear hierarchy is worked out but instead of relaxation techniques, the child is asked to imagine that the graded exposure trials are taking place with the help of his or her favourite hero or heroine. An imagined adventure story is constructed in which child and hero progressively overcome the stages of the fear hierarchy.

Contingency management

Another form of therapy that may be used with phobic children. It attempts to teach the child a new 'target behaviour' in the presence of the phobic stimulus to replace the usual fear response. A series of target behaviours may be needed. This is accomplished by using positive reinforcement methods (i.e. rewards that the child desires) each time a target behaviour is achieved.

Modelling

A process in which a therapist first demonstrates or

'models' a treatment task while the patient watches. The therapist then assists the patient to accomplish the task himself.

Single-session treatments (see Chapter 9)

An intensive session of graduated exposure lasting for a period of about three hours used as a one-off treatment for specific phobias.

Self-efficacy training and guided mastery

A therapeutic approach that emphasises the gradual acquisition of skills and strategies by the patient while in the phobic situation. Mastering these skills enables the person to realise that he can, in fact, exercise control while confronting the phobic situation.

The performance tasks are set by the therapist, who accompanies, aids and guides the patient and helps him to achieve them. However, as soon as possible, the therapist begins to decrease his level of support (which may mean physical removal and giving instructions from some distance away) so that assistance is minimal and the person learns to believe in his own capabilities.

Social skills training and assertiveness training

These are techniques that may be used, generally in conjunction with other therapies, in the treatment of social phobia and agoraphobia. The techniques

232

employed involve instructing the patient in certain procedures such as the exchange of greetings and practising the skills in role play and in real life.

Relaxation and breathing training

This involves teaching a phobic person relaxation techniques and breathing exercises to counteract some of the physical symptoms of fear.

Many of the alternative therapies described in Chapter 24 may be helpful in this area. However, in the clinical setting, relaxation and breathing techniques are always used in conjunction with other therapies.

Cognitive-based therapies

Cognitive therapies aim to manipulate and alter a phobic person's mistaken, irrational beliefs about the feared stimulus.

Rational-emotive therapy

This therapy teaches the patient ways of 'arguing with himself' to challenge his own stated beliefs.

Self-instructional training

This is based on the use of a series of positive instructions or statements that the person first repeats out loud as a means of confronting phobic fear.

These statements concern various aspects of the phobia such as preparing to confront the feared stimulus, imaginal confrontation, coping with the situation and reinforcement of the person's ability to cope (self-efficacy).

Paradoxical intention

This is a method in which a phobic person is encouraged to greatly exaggerate his fear and the circumstances in which the phobia occurs in order ` to, paradoxically, diminish the power of the phobia.

This is a light-hearted approach, the exaggeration often being to a ridiculous extent designed to generate humour, and is generally used in conjunction with other therapies.

Cognitive—behavioural therapies

As previously mentioned, many modern treatment programmes combine behavioural and cognitive approaches, usually incorporating some form of exposure therapy.

Pharmacological treatments for phobias

It is widely accepted by most experts that pharmacological treatments are not helpful to people suffering from specific phobias. However, medication has been used in the treatment of agoraphobia and social phobias, often aimed at relieving panic symptoms or the visible, physical signs of performance anxiety. Three classes of drugs have been used in the treatment of phobia:

1. Antidepressants
2. Benzodiazepines
3. Beta-blockers.

Both traditional and new varieties have been tried, generally with mixed results.

Antidepressants

Antidepressants , at least in the short term, have a lower risk of producing dependency and withdrawal symptoms. However, they have to be taken for some time before they start to work and can produce unpleasant side effects which may make them unpopular with patients. They do, however, seem to relieve the panic symptoms of a significant number of phobic patients.

Benzodiazepines

Benzodiazepines begin to act immediately and have also been shown to provide relief for some phobic patients in lessening panic and anxiety symptoms.

However, they quickly produce dependency and withdrawal symptoms and so they are generally cautiously prescribed for short-term use.

Understandably, phobic patients may be reluctant to take a drug that carries the attached risk of dependency.

Beta-blockers

Beta-blockers produce fewer side effects and have proved effective in some phobic patients in relieving the physical symptoms of 'performance' and social anxiety. They do not appear to be helpful in treating panic symptoms.

One of the main areas of concern is that all of these drugs are potent chemical agents which can cause side effects and, in some cases, dependency and withdrawal symptoms. A second area of concern, in addition to those discussed above, is the risk of relapse or the return of intense phobic symptoms once medication is discontinued.

Several studies have shown that this is a very real risk and for this reason some clinicians have tried combining pharmacological treatment with psychological behavioural therapy. It appears that combined therapy is generally more effective than drug treatment alone.

However, there is also little evidence that combined therapy is superior to psychological therapies on their own. Given the undoubted problems attached to taking potent psychotropic drugs, it would seem that these should continue to be used very cautiously in the treatment of phobias and only in the most severely affected patients. Hence psychological therapies provide the best form of treatment for the great majority of phobic people.

Chapter 23
Stress

Many phobics can become extremely stressed as a result of living with a phobic fear and there are many alternative therapies that can help them to become more relaxed (*see* Chapter 24) but by way of an introduction to alternative therapies, this chapter looks at what is understood by stress in a little more detail.

Stress has been part of the human condition since the beginning of time and is an integral factor in human survival. It is an active force that helps people to rise to meet whatever challenges everyday life may throw at them.

The body's response to stress is fast and effective, going into what can best be described as 'fright, fight or flight' mode. This means that when a person registers a challenge, his system undergoes a chain reaction of responses, which flood the body with enough strength and energy to either fight or take flight.

This reaction has been a factor in human motivation since the earliest stages of evolutionary history (*see* Chapter 21). Primitive human beings frequently faced life and death situations, when alertness, strength, speed and performance were vital and the primary, instinctive response was to survive. The type of challenges met with today, however, are rather different and, as they rarely require a physical response, the body's reaction to the situation is often inappropriate.

Also, the stresses of modern life are more complex and last over longer periods of time. In the past, challenges had to be resolved instantaneously; today, people are subjected to long-term emotional, occupational and environmental anxieties, which keep them in an almost perpetual state of fight or flight.

It is vital, therefore, that people, including the phobic patient, make a priority of finding ways of easing their bodies and minds out of fight or flight mode and in order to do this they need a greater understanding and awareness of how their bodies work.

Stress – the body's response

The body's automatic physical response to danger or stress involves an intricate chain reaction of bodily and biochemical effects, involving the brain, the nervous system and hormones. As soon as a threat is perceived, the body explodes with energy and strength, and thousands of messenger hormones flood into the bloodstream to call the alarm. Minds and bodies instantly become clear, alert and poised – ready for action.

In this alarm reaction, the main players are the lungs, brain, nervous system, muscle systems and hormones. Arousal is initially registered by the hypothalamus – a tiny crowd of cells at the base of the brain – which controls all automatic bodily functions and reactions. It releases chemicals, called endorphins, that act as natural painkillers. They dull the perception of pain and mental turmoil and help people to deal with the situation by blocking out factors that may otherwise prevent individuals from giving less than their peak performance.

Another chemical, called adrenaline, causes a quickening of the heart rate, a raising of blood pressure and a release of vital nutrients. It also creates muscle tension and affects breathing patterns, making them faster and shallower. Adrenaline is only one of the arousal hormones released by the adrenal gland near the kidneys: noradrenaline, associated with positive ecstatic arousal, is also released into the bloodstream; the hormone cortisol is the agent involved in converting glycogen, stored in the liver, into blood sugar, creating instant energy and alerting the brain; and the required surge of strength and effort comes from the male hormone, testosterone.

The thyroid gland also plays a part in the body's response. It releases thyroxin, a hormone that stimulates the metabolic system, increasing its work rate and regulating oxygen consumption. This is vital, as the body anticipates that it will need increased resources of energy. The digestive system also slows down during this process, as blood is diverted from the skin and stomach. The body instinctively shuts down the unnecessary systems in order to concentrate on mobilising those vital for survival. As the digestive system is not deemed essential in a life or death situation, it slows down and is effectively put on hold.

The body has undoubtedly evolved an efficient and prompt survival response but, as already mentioned, the causes of stress today are more complex and require more sophisticated solutions over a longer period of time. The body's hormonal system suffers if it stays in fight mode, as lengthy periods with our bodies on red-alert are not healthy for our mental or physical wellbeing, and what begins as a positive range of responses can eventually have a negative effect on health.

Research shows that a person may not realise that his body is on challenge alert. For example, without being aware of it, emotions such as anger, anxiety and impatience produce the same chemical reactions in the body as standing in front of a speeding car. The same physiology that leaves a person feeling poised and alert, can create havoc over a long period of time. Such a build-up of energy can lead people to become stress addicts hooked on the adrenaline rush that stressful situations create. People can become so used to living on such a psychological and physical 'tilt' that they no longer realise the harm this is causing.

Overdoses of adrenaline can cause irritability and agitation, while too much noradrenaline can leave a person feeling disconnected and high. If arousal continues, the adrenal glands create anti-inflammatory chemicals to speed tissue repair but cortisol will also suppress the immune system, leaving it vulnerable to illness and disease.

Extra sodium is retained, endangering the performance of the cardiovascular system by causing fluid retention, raising the heart rate, increasing blood pressure and possibly inducing blood clots. Stomach ulcers are a classic symptom of stress, as the stomach cannot deal with the extra secretion of acid that occurs during times of turbulence. Acute and cumulative stress over a period of time can even cause death.

Less drastic but very common symptoms of stress include:

- increased pupil dilation
- perspiration
- increased heart rate and blood pressure (to get more blood to the muscles, brain and heart)
- rapid breathing (to take in more oxygen)
- muscle tenseness (in preparation for action)
- increased blood flow to the brain, heart and muscles (the organs that are most important in dealing with danger)
- less blood flow to the skin, digestive tract, kidneys and liver (where it is least needed in times of crisis)

- increased mental alertness and sensitivity (to assess the situation and act quickly)
- increased blood sugar, fats and cholesterol (for extra energy)
- a rise in platelets and blood-clotting factors (to prevent haemorrhage in case of injury)

This only accounts for the physical dangers of prolonged stress. The effects on emotional and psychological wellbeing can be devastating, causing depression, anxiety, disorientation, panic, anger, insecurity and frustration. Family breakdown, mental illness, alcoholism and drug dependency can all be caused by an accumulation of stress.

The relaxation response

Just as the body has an automatic process to prepare it for a fight or flight situation, it can also go into what is called the 'relaxation response'. This stage of low arousal is less well known than the body's red-alert status, and it initially takes a concentrated effort in order to experience it. The symptoms of the fight or flight response – increased metabolic rate, quickened heart rate and faster breathing – are the direct opposite of those experienced by the body while in a state of deep relaxation.

A person needs to be truly relaxed for the process to begin and for the body to feel the full benefits. Two branches of the autonomic nervous system are responsible for most of the changes that take place.

What is known as the sympathetic branch slows down, allowing the parasympathetic branch to assume a greater role, calming the body and mind and decreasing metabolism until it reaches a hypometabolic state as opposed to the hypermetabolic state experienced during the fight or flight process.

During relaxation, the body requires very low maintenance, and the decrease in metabolism is similar only to that found in deep sleep. Breathing becomes more regular and the heart rate decreases. In a sustained period of relaxation, oxygen consumption actually falls below that measured during deep sleep. There is also a significant fall in blood lactate, a substance that enters the blood through the metabolism of skeletal muscles. This occurs three times faster during meditation, for example, than while sitting at rest. Blood pressure is also lowered, but only to normal pre-stress levels. All this allows the body to recover from the strains placed on it by the stress of everyday life.

The relaxation response also elicits a marked alteration in brain activity. The brain emits four types of waves, each with its own rhythm: beta waves signify everyday conscious rhythms; delta waves are present during sleep; theta waves appear while in a dreamlike state; and alpha waves are more prominent when the mind is active, yet relaxed. Effective meditation manufactures a predominance of alpha and theta waves – signifying a state of restfulness and deep relaxation, where the mind is alert but not strained or confused. These waves appear almost as soon as the body starts to relax, increasing in frequency as the process intensifies and allowing clearer and more constructive thinking.

A prolonged period of relaxation will also increase the body's secretion of particular mood-altering chemicals, known as neurotransmitters. One of these, serotonin, is a powerful hormone that is associated with feelings of happiness and contentment. By easing his body and mind out of a state of stress and into this state of relaxation, the phobic person will be more able to deal successfully with his phobic fear.

Chapter 24
Alternative Therapies

Many of the so-called alternative therapies, which do not lie under the umbrella of orthodox medicine, may offer help to a phobic person. This is because most offer methods of achieving relaxation as a means of counteracting stress and anxiety and this can be immensely beneficial to phobia sufferers. In most cases, the phobic fear itself is not being targeted directly but rather the person's general levels of anxiety and stress.

Alternative therapies adopt a gentle, holistic approach aimed at enhancing a sense of wellbeing and a state of relaxation and, if a phobic person is able to feel generally more relaxed and less anxious, it has a positive effect on his self-esteem and overall health and so he is better equipped to deal with his phobia. Hence, although they may not provide a cure, these therapeutic methods are highly suitable on their own or as additional techniques in a treatment programme.

Acupressure

A traditional form of oriental healing, combining elements of acupuncture and massage. It utilises the same pressure points that are used in acupuncture to balance the flow of healing energy, qi, within the body, but massage, usually with the fingers and thumb, is applied instead of the insertion of needles. It may be helpful in relieving symptoms of stress, anxiety and depression and so can be of benefit to phobic patients.

Acupuncture

Acupuncture is an ancient Chinese therapy that involves inserting needles into the skin at specific points of the body which are located along 'meridians'. These are the pathways or energy channels that are believed to be connected to the internal organs of the body. The energy, qi, and the needles, (sometimes aided by the use of electrical currents and even laser beams), are used to decrease or increase the flow of qi or to unblock it if it is impeded.

Traditional Chinese medicine holds that the body contains two, opposing natural forces known as yin and yang and that imbalances of one or other of these is responsible for diseases and ailments. Acupuncture aims to establish whether there is an imbalance between yin and yang and then restore it by the insertion of needles at the correct, specific points.

There are several factors that can change the flow of qi and they may be of an emotional, physical or environmental nature. Painful conditions can be relieved by acupuncture but also symptoms of stress and anxiety. Hence acupuncture can be of benefit to phobia sufferers and is a type of therapy that has become increasingly popular in Western countries.

Aromatherapy

Aromatherapy is a method of healing using very concentrated essential oils that are often highly aromatic and are extracted from plants. Constituents of the oils produce the characteristic odour or perfume given off by the plant. Essential oils help the plant in some way to complete its cycle of growth and reproduction and different parts may produce their own form of oil.

Plant essences have been used throughout the ages to aid healing and in recent years there has been a great rekindling of interest in the practice of aromatherapy, with many people turning to this form of treatment. The most familiar method of treatment associated with aromatherapy is massage using various combinations of essential oils. Other methods that may be recommended for use at home include bathing with appropriate oils added to the water.

An aromatherapist is able to design a whole body massage for an individual person, choosing the essential oils that are most suited to the person's temperament, symptoms and medical or emotional problems. Aromatherapy is of great benefit in relieving stress and stress-related symptoms including anxiety, depression and insomnia. Hence it is entirely suitable for the general treatment of phobia, enhancing a feeling of wellbeing and relaxation and reducing general anxiety.

Art therapy

Art therapy is aimed at helping people with emotional and psychological problems, particularly those who find it difficult to communicate verbally. The creative media of art and craft are used to help the person express his innermost thoughts and fears. An art therapist is a trained psychotherapist who is also qualified in the creative arts. Therapy often takes place in a group setting and the role of the therapist is to give guidance, be a supportive listener and to help each person discuss his work and through this, talk about himself and his fears.

It is not necessary to be good at art to take part in art therapy. Often, it is just a case of rediscovering the creativity which lies within each person that is easily expressed in childhood but tends to get suppressed in adult life. Art therapy can be of considerable help to phobia sufferers although, unfortunately, it is not easily available in the British Isles.

Autogenic training

Autogenic training is a form of therapy that seeks to teach a patient to relax, thereby relieving stress. Patients with a variety of disorders may benefit from autogenic training, including those suffering from phobias, anxiety, depression, insomnia and some other psychological illnesses.

This form of therapy can benefit people of all age groups, although it is considered that children under the age of six years may not be able to understand the training.

Therapists in autogenic training usually hold medical or nursing qualifications and expect to obtain a full picture of the patient's state of health before treatment begins.

Training involves teaching the patient a series of six basic exercises that can be undertaken either lying flat on the back, sitting in an armchair or sitting towards the edge of a chair with the head bent forwards and the chin on the chest. The six exercises concentrate on:

- breathing and respiration
- heartbeat
- the forehead to induce a feeling of warmness
- the lower abdomen and stomach to induce a feeling of warmth
- the neck, shoulders, arms and legs to induce a feeling of heaviness.

By learning these exercises and other techniques, the person is helped to achieve a state of relaxation and tranquility, sleep more restfully and enjoy an enhanced feeling of wellbeing, all of which is helpful in the general treatment of phobia.

Autosuggestion or Couéism

A form of self-help based on meditation and the release of the body's own healing forces which are mediated through the power of the mind. It is usually used in conjunction with other therapies. Autosuggestion can be beneficial to those suffering from most forms of physical illness, as well as psychological and emotional conditions and problems and it works by harnessing the power of mind over matter.

It was developed by a French doctor, Emile Coué (1857–1926), and his ideas were ridiculed at first. However, the power of the mind to promote healing is now widely accepted, acknowledged and encouraged throughout the medical world, both in the treatment of physical and mental disorders. Coué developed the phrase 'Every day, in every way, I am getting better and better' which was destined to become famous.

The technique itself is simple; the person chooses a time when he is feeling relaxed such as on first waking up in the morning. He tries to empty his mind of all distracting thoughts and repeats a simple phrase (either Coué's or another that is suitable) over and over again, either silently or out loud.

251

In the treatment of phobia, a suitable phrase can be worked out which helps the person to lessen or overcome his fear. The technique needs to be practised once or twice each day for as long as necessary and it is generally considered to be a safe and helpful form of treatment which enhances feelings of self-control and wellbeing.

Bach remedies

A series of 38 remedies obtained from spring water in which certain flowers have been floated under direct sunlight. Each remedy is said to correspond to a particular mental or emotional state and they can be bought over the counter at health food shops.

The remedies are designed to be used as a self-help measure and the idea is for the patient to honestly appraise his mental state and select the remedies that most nearly correspond to this.

It is best to take no more than five remedies at any one time and, if necessary, to experiment to see which is most useful. Bach remedies are suitable for individuals suffering from phobias, since they are based upon psychological and emotional factors and many people find them very helpful.

Psychotherapists believe that the process of self-examination and taking steps to help oneself are of great value to phobic patients.

Bioenergetic therapy

Bioenergetic therapy is based on the idea that there is a flow of energy between the body and the mind that affects both physical and mental wellbeing. It is thought that psychological problems and emotions such as fear and anxiety affect the person's physical state such as causing muscle tension, poor posture, inefficient breathing, etc. A series of exercises are practised that include breathing techniques that free the body so that the energy force can flow more naturally and the psychological or emotional problem is eased. Discussion also forms part of the programme.

In general, bioenergetics is practised in a group setting, following an individual assessment, usually as part of a broader programme of therapy. Many people report positive benefits from bioenergetics, especially that they feel that they have more energy and a greater sense of wellbeing. These aspects, along with the benefits that come from learning to breathe correctly and discussing problems with others, can be helpful to people who suffer from phobias.

Colour therapy

In orthodox medicine, it is accepted that colours exert subtle influences on people especially affecting their state of mind and psychological wellbeing. It is well known that human beings respond to coloured light and are affected in different ways by rays of various wavelengths. This even occurs in people who are blind. So the human body is able to respond in subtle ways to electromagnetic radiation. Colour therapists believe that each individual receives and absorbs electromagnetic radiation from the sun and emits it in a unique 'aura' – a pattern of colours peculiar to that person.

It is believed that the aura can be recorded on film by a photographic technique known as Kirlian photography. If disorder is present, caused by physical or psychological conditions, it manifests itself as a disturbance of the vibrations that form the aura, giving a distorted pattern. During a consultation, a colour therapist pays particular attention to the patient's spine as each individual vertebra is believed to be related to one of the eight colours of the visible spectrum. The eight colours are repeated in their usual sequence from the top to the base of the spine.

The treatment consists of bathing the body in coloured light, with appropriate colours being decided upon by the therapist. Usually one main colour is used along with a complementary one and the light is emitted in irregular bursts. Treatment sessions last for a little less than 20 minutes and are continued for at least seven weeks. The aim is to restore the natural balance in the pattern of the aura and the therapist also advises the person on the use of colours in the home to enhance health and wellbeing.

Colour therapy is designed to be used in conjunction with orthodox methods. It is a gentle therapy that may be helpful to some phobic patients, particularly those who feel that colour may be a factor in their phobia.

Dance movement therapy

Dance movement therapy is aimed at helping people to resolve deep-seated problems by communicating with, and relating to, others through the medium of physical movements and dance. The ability to express deep, inner feelings in 'body language' and physical movements is innate in human beings. Young children express themselves freely in this way and without inhibition, and dancing would appear to be common to all past and present races and tribes of people. In modern industrial societies, however, many people find themselves unable to communicate their problems and fears either verbally or physically and may repress them to such an extent that they become ill.

Dance movement therapy aims to help people to explore, recognise and come to terms with feelings and problems that they usually repress and to communicate them to others. This therapy is of particular benefit to those suffering from emotional, psychological and stress-related disorders and anxiety and can be helpful to those who are phobic. Children are, in particular, often very receptive to dance movement therapy.

People of any age can take part in this therapy as the aim is to explore gently physical movements that lie within each person's capabilities. The therapist may suggest movements, but aims to encourage patients to learn to take the initiative. Therapy usually takes place in a group setting and eventually, members learn to talk over feelings and problems that have emerged and suggest ways of resolving them.

Dance movement therapy is another approach that may help a phobic person in a number of ways – through exploring hidden feelings, interacting with others who have problems and through doing something positive to help himself.

Exercise

Exercise would not normally be considered an alternative therapy since it should form part of a person's normal life activities but sadly this is not the case. It is impossible to overestimate the significance of exercise in a healthy and relaxed lifestyle. If a body is never pushed beyond its regular pace, relaxation periods will invariably have less benefit. Exercise does not just promote an increase in physical fitness; people who exercise regularly can enjoy a range of secondary benefits.

Regular exercise improves sleep, reduces headaches, creates a feeling of wellbeing, and increases concentration and stamina. Endorphins are released into the brain during exercise and these chemicals promote a sense of positivity and happiness that will last for some time after the actual activity. This is an effective tool in the fight against the stress experienced by the phobic patient and a vital move in the preparation for a more relaxed life.

In today's society, there is a general emphasis on sedentary lifestyles, and it is a trend that shows little sign of slowing down. This makes it difficult to find an appropriate outlet for mental negativity and accumulated physical frustration. Physical exertion is perfect for releasing the toxic emotions that threaten a relaxed sense of wellbeing. Tension, anger, frustration and aggression can be worked out of the system as a person exercises mental muscles along with physical ones.

Exercise is a personal thing and different people will prefer one kind of exercise over another. Preferences will be affected by an individual's personality, physical capabilities and time available. Realistically, tailoring a physical activity to a person's lifestyle is the best way to ensure that the exercise is kept up. Even as little as twenty minutes a day put aside for such activities will be of great benefit.

It is always a good idea to seek advice on which form of sport to take up and to consult a doctor before beginning. Also remember that the body benefits more from short periods of regular exercise than from infrequent bursts. Two suitable activities include walking and running.

Walking

Walking is often overlooked as an activity. A brisk, purposeful walk improves muscle condition, circulation and posture. All that is needed is a good pair of strong shoes and a lightweight, waterproof jacket for wetter days. Anyone walking for the first time should walk for thirty minutes a day and walk fast enough to become a little out of breath. The walking route should be varied so that it does not consist of flat ground all the time. After a week or two, the walking time can be increased to about forty-five minutes. By then, the benefits, such as sleeping better, sharper concentration and feeling more balanced emotionally, should be quite noticeable.

Walking is an ideal exercise because it can be done almost anywhere – in the country or the city. Walking briskly every day brings about a fit body, glowing skin and a new sense of wellbeing.

Running

Running is a most satisfying form of exercise for many people. No special training is needed although it makes sense to follow a running programme which gradually works towards the runner being able to run for half and hour or more without stopping. As with walking it can be done anywhere – at home or on holiday. All that is needed is a good pair of running shoes and the self-discipline to get started. It is important to check fitness before starting a running programme. In particular, it is a good idea for anyone who has a family history of heart disease or who has been recently ill to have a doctor's check-up just to make sure that running is a safe activity for them.

Runners who can run for half an hour or so without stopping, often experience a kind of euphoria known as 'runner's high', which is one of the reasons that running is such a good tool for anyone seeking relaxation in the deepest sense of the word. Having run until their legs are beginning to feel heavy and breathing is hard, many runners suddenly feel as if they could run on and on. Perceptions are heightened and, as the mind clears, problems are seen in their proper perspective. This does not happen during every run, but it is an experience well worth working towards.

Herbal medicine

Herbal medicine is the use of herbs and plants to prevent and treat disease. The medicinal use of herbs is believed to be as old as mankind with written records dating back, for example, to the time of ancient Egypt. By the Middle Ages in Europe, *Herbals* (books recording plants and their medicinal properties) were being compiled. Many apothecaries collected and kept a supply of plants to make their own remedies and monasteries each had their own herb garden, the monks themselves being skilled in the arts of healing.

Herbal medicine declined in the nineteenth and twentieth centuries with the advent of modern medicine and pharmacology. However, in recent years there has been a tremendous rekindling of interest in the use of plant remedies, not only among herbal enthusiasts but in doctors and scientists as well. It is now widely recognised that most of the traditional plant remedies have healing properties that can stand up to scientific scrutiny. Also, the race is on to halt the inexorable rise in plant extinctions as it is recognised that species are being lost that could prove to be of immense benefit to mankind.

Herbal medicine is acknowledged today as being a helpful and natural method of preventing and treating illness and of promoting good health. It can be particularly beneficial to those suffering from emotional and psychological disorders, including anxiety, and so is well suited to help victims of phobia. A herbalist has extensive knowledge of the many different plant remedies available and prescribes those which are best suited to an individual patient, following a thorough health assessment. However, many of the preparations are also available as over-the-counter remedies from health food stores and chemists or from mail order catalogues.

Some of the preparations that are particularly useful in alleviating anxiety are those made from lemon balm, lime flowers, valerian, borage, hops, chamomile and lavender. Herbal remedies are generally considered to be a safe and gentle form of treatment that has proved helpful to some phobia sufferers.

Homeopathy

The aim of homeopathy is to cure an illness or disorder by treating the whole person rather than merely concentrating on a set of symptoms. Hence, in homeopathy the approach is holistic and the overall state of health of the patient, especially his or her emotional and psychological wellbeing, is regarded as being significant. A homeopath notes the symptoms that the person wishes to have cured but also takes time to discover other signs or indications of disorder that the patient may regard as being less important.

The reasoning behind this is that illness is a sign of disorder or imbalance within the body. It is believed that the whole 'make-up' of a person determines, to a great extent, the type of disorders to which that individual is prone and the symptoms likely to occur. A homeopathic remedy must be suitable both for the symptoms and the characteristics and temperament of the patient. Hence, two patients with the same illness may be offered different remedies according to their individual natures and one remedy may also be used to treat different groups of symptoms or ailments.

Homeopathic remedies are derived from plant, animal and mineral sources and are prescribed on the basis of an ancient philosophy, first formulated by Hippocrates in the fifth century BC that 'like cures like'. The idea was revived by Samuel Hahnemann in the nineteenth century, who found that giving an extremely minute dose of a substance that stimulated symptoms of an illness in a healthy person could then be used to fight that illness in someone who was sick.

Since the philosophy underlying homeopathy centres on the whole person, with particular emphasis on psychological and emotional factors, it is an eminently suitable therapy for people suffering from phobias. A homeopath draws upon extensive experience to prescribe remedies best suited to each individual person, following a thorough discussion with the patient.

Some of the remedies that might be prescribed for phobias are *Aconitum napellus*, *Arsenicum album*, *Argentum nitricum* and *Pulsatilla nigricans*. Homeopathic remedies are used in extremely dilute amounts and it is believed that their curative properties are enhanced by successive dilutions. There are many people who find homeopathy helpful and it is a gentle therapy which can be used alone or in conjunction with a treatment programme.

Humanistic psychology and psychotherapy

The philosophy behind humanistic psychology is that each individual is ultimately responsible for his own behaviour and possesses the ability within himself to change and to undergo personal growth. Hence factors such as one's environment, upbringing and current family and social circumstances are held to be largely insignificant.

A humanistic psychotherapist tries to help the patient or client bring about the changes that the person has himself identified as being important. The therapist does this by being willing to discuss ideas, make suggestions and encourage the client to develop his own ways of bringing about change.

People with emotional and psychological problems can be helped by the humanistic psychotherapeutic approach. Many psychotherapists believe that the processes of self-examination, along with developing self-confidence and self-reliance, are of value to people with phobias. Humanistic psychotherapy may be able to help phobic people to retain the gains that they achieved during or following a treatment programme.

Hypnotherapy

Hypnotherapy is the process of inducing a trance-like state in a patient in order to bring about a desirable and positive change in the person's physical or mental health. Under hypnosis, the mind and body become able to undergo healing changes that appear to be less accessible in the conscious state. People with a wide range of physical and emotional disorders, addictions (for example, to smoking) and sufferers from phobia have been helped by hypnotherapy. However, it is necessary for the patient to fully trust the therapist, to have complete confidence in the process and to co-operate fully and the technique may not be suitable for everyone.

Massage

As long ago as 3000 BC, massage was used as a therapy in the Far East, making it one of the oldest-known treatments used by mankind. In the year 5 BC in ancient Greece, the physician Hippocrates recommended that in order to maintain good health, a massage using oils should be administered daily after a perfumed bath. Hence the relaxation and healing powers of massage have been recognised for at least 5,000 years.

Massage increased in popularity during the nineteenth century when the technique which became known as Swedish massage was introduced. Much more recently, during the 1970s, a new overall technique of massage was developed in which the underlying aim was to address the person's whole state, both physical and psychological.

Also combined in this form of therapeutic massage were methods borrowed from reflexology and shiatsu with the overall aim of combining relaxation, stimulation and invigoration to promote good health. This massage is commonly used to induce general relaxation so that tensions, stress and anxiety can be eased and eliminated. It promotes a feeling of calmness and serenity and this is particularly beneficial to people suffering from anxiety or depression or phobia. It leaves people feeling generally relaxed and this increases self-confidence and ability to deal with problems. Hence, massage can be of considerable benefit to phobic people and it would usually be used as part of a treatment programme.

Four basic techniques are used in massage: percussion (or drumming or tapotement); friction (also called pressure); effleurage (also called stroking); and petrissage (also called kneading). The masseur or masseuse is a skilled person who first takes time to discover a full picture of the patient's overall state of health, including any physical problems. A massage programme is then worked out that is best suited to the needs of the individual patient.

Meditation

Through meditation it is possible to achieve a state of passive alertness that transcends the everyday level of thought and distraction. Achieving this higher level of consciousness may at first seem a difficult proposition, but with practice and effort it is something everyone can do. Some people are put off by the image of meditation as something steeped in impenetrable Eastern mysticism, but meditators do not have to submerge themselves in religious or spiritual teaching to gain from this art. Meditation is really a very simple way of lightening the mind, forgetting about everyday stresses and concentrating solely on mental relaxation

The effect of meditation on the body

Meditation has several effects on the body. As well as slowing down the heart rate, it can significantly reduce the oxygen consumption and carbon dioxide production of meditators. Within a few minutes of starting to meditate these can fall up to twenty per cent below normal levels. During meditation there is also a reduction of activity in the nervous system. The parasympathetic branch of the autonomic nervous system (the branch responsible for calming us down) dominates. During meditation the body achieves what is called a hypometabolic state. This is best described as 'deep and prolonged relaxation'.

Practised regularly (for around twenty to thirty minutes each day) meditation helps fight depression, reduce hypertension and relieve anxiety. Research also shows that concentration, memory and creativity are improved through regular sessions of meditation.

How to begin

When starting to meditate it is important to find a quiet, peaceful area and to use the same place regularly. Some people find it useful to contemplate an object as they meditate. Traditionally, a single flower or a flickering flame is used but it is entirely up to the individual – whatever concentrates the mind and helps to clear it of clutter. Soft background music (for example, environmental music that features the sound of waterfalls, rain or birdsong), incense and low lights are some the tools which help to create a conducive atmosphere.

Posture is very important in meditation. An easy posture to adopt consists of sitting cross-legged with both feet on the floor. The back should be straight but not tense and the stomach muscles relaxed. With the muscles of the lower back bearing the weight of the body and with the head, neck and trunk in line, the centre of gravity passes from the base of the spine right through the top of the head. The hands can either rest lightly on the knees or be held in the lap, either one on top of the other or clasped lightly.

Breathing is also central to effective meditation. Breathing well is an excellent way of focusing the mind and blocking out the surface 'chatter' of the mind. In order to achieve this, sit in your chosen position and relax your entire body.

Once your eyes are closed, relax and focus on the rhythm of your breathing. It will probably be shallower and slower than usual at first. Slowly deepen your intake of air and watch your stomach rise and fall with each breath. Count each one, saying to yourself 'in' with each inhalation and 'out' with each exhalation. Don't try to push the pace; let it emerge naturally. Slowly you will find yourself focusing entirely on your own breathing. In time this should help to banish other thoughts from your mind.

Which method?

There are many different meditation techniques or methods. Some have been handed down from generation to generation for thousands of years and remain in their pure form. Others have been adapted to suit current circumstances. Deciding which method is the right one can be quite bewildering but it is worth remembering that the techniques or methods are not the ends in themselves – they are the motorway on which the journey to meditation moves.

Mantras

Repeating a word or phrase – a mantra – over and over again is probably the most practised and widespread path to meditation and one of the oldest. The mantra may be chanted aloud or repeated silently. Focusing on a mantra during meditation can lead to some of the deepest and most profound of meditation sessions.

Most of the major religions have their own mantra, as in the Hindu *Hare Krishna*: or 'Hail to Krishna'. For those who wish to use a mantra in their meditation but who want to avoid religion, any word or phrase, no matter how meaningless, will do.

Many people take up meditation simply to relax but the more experienced they become, the more far-reaching are their aims, and they feel themselves drawn to the more mystical side of meditation – the search for an understanding of the nature of reality. The deeper they search, the calmer, happier and more satisfied they become.

Metamorphic technique

Massage and manipulation of the feet, hands and top of the head which, it is felt, releases inner, healing energy from within the body. The technique is said to help those with emotional and psychological problems or who have persistent health disorders. Practitioners of the technique hold that they act merely as agents for healing changes that are brought about from within the patient. The aim is to help the patient to help himself and the exercises can be learned so that family members can practise them on each other. The metamorphic technique is a gentle form of mind-body massage therapy that may be helpful to phobic patients.

Naturopathy

Naturopathy is a combination of different methods of natural healing that are extremely wide-ranging, and a practitioner may become a specialist in one particular area. Although naturopathy can be used to treat the symptoms of an illness it is, fundamentally, a way of life and a means of disease prevention. The management of stress and anxiety is a particular area that is addressed by naturopathy and adopting a healthy, naturopathic lifestyle benefits everybody and can be helpful to those suffering from phobias.

The principle therapeutic elements of naturopathy are:

1. The examination of nutrition and diet including the use of vitamin and mineral supplements.
2. Detoxification – the use of short periods of fasting or controlled diets and supplements to aid the natural processes by which the body rids itself of toxic substances.
3. Ways and means to control and reduce stress and anxiety including recognising and eliminating the cause whenever possible, relaxation techniques, modification of diet and the use of supplements, particularly to support the adrenal gland.
4. Hydrotherapy – the use of water to promote healing.
5. Herbal medicine
6. Homeopathy
7. Physical therapies such as massage, chiropractic and osteopathy
8. Counselling and lifestyle modification, which can be of particular value in relieving psychological, behavioural and emotional problems as well as physical ailments. Treatment may include hypnotherapy, relaxation techniques, visualisation (image) therapy, colour, music or

dance therapy in addition to other naturopathic methods.

9. The use of acupuncture and Oriental therapies such as shiatsu, yoga and T'ai Chi Ch'uan

10. Exercise – the importance of exercise in the promotion of good health, including psychological and emotional wellbeing, and in the treatment of ailments is recognised by naturopaths and forms a part of most therapeutic programmes.

A naturopath is interested in the person as a whole and not just in a particular condition or set of symptoms that may be troubling the patient. Hence consulting a naturopath gives a person the chance to discuss every aspect of life with someone who is concerned to offer help.

Each naturopath is likely to have developed his or her own particular approach to overcoming health problems, but in most cases, including those of phobia, they will suggest diet and lifestyle changes along with other therapeutic methods from the list above.

Psychosynthesis

A process of self-growth and self-development to achieve, in some sense, a new and better identity. It is said to be helpful to those suffering from various anxiety and stress-related disorders, including phobias and usually requires about six treatment sessions, guided by a therapist. During these sessions, self-analysis, imaginal and visualisation techniques and meditation are among the techniques that may be employed.

Reflexology

Reflexology is a technique of diagnosis and treatment in which certain areas of the body, particularly the feet, are massaged to alleviate pain or other symptoms in the organs of the body. It is thought to have originated about five thousand years ago in China and was also used by the ancient Egyptians.

It was introduced to Western society by Dr William Fitzgerald, an American physician. He applied ten zones (or energy channels) to the surface of the body, hence the term 'zone therapy' was applied, and these zones or channels were considered to be paths along which a person's vital energy or energy force flowed. The zones were considered to end at the hands and feet.

Subsequent practitioners of reflexology have concentrated primarily on the feet, although the working of reflexes throughout the body can be beneficial. Reflexology is not only able to help physical disorders but psychological and emotional ones as well. It may be helpful to some phobia sufferers and many people find reflexology massage to be soothing and relaxing.

Breathing techniques

These usually involve carrying out various exercises to relax muscles or to reinstate correct breathing, both of which tend to be compromised in people who are highly anxious and fearful, such as those suffering from phobias. Usually this involves becoming aware that the diaphragm should be involved in breathing since, in most cases, adults rely on the chest and rib cage to force air into and out of the lungs.

In chest breathing, the process is rapid and shallow and the lungs fail to empty properly and this is the method resorted to at times of physical and psychological stress. However, if used continually it becomes a cause of stress in itself, and this is a particular risk for phobic people, many of whom tend to hyperventilate or breathe wrongly as a result of extreme fear.

In order to restore correct breathing, the person must learn to recognise the presence and operation of the diaphragm which is a membrane of muscle and tendon separating the thoracic and abdominal cavities. The diaphragm bulges up into its resting position during exhalation, forcing air out of the lungs as it moves upwards into the chest cavity.

One way of becoming aware of its activity is to breathe in and out deeply, beyond the normal point, to force air in and out of the 'dead space' in the lungs. During inspiration the diaphragm flattens, thereby reducing pressure in the thoracic cavity and drawing air in to fill the lungs completely.

This ensures that a good supply of oxygen enters the blood and tissues and that there is efficient elimination of carbon dioxide. Efficient breathing using the diaphragm helps to lower blood pressure and directly relieves anxiety, tension and stress. Other breathing exercises may take various forms, often concentrating on slow, regular controlled breathing, perhaps in time with counting, to help counteract the tendency to hyperventilate in situations of anxiety or panic.

Rogerian therapy

A form of humanistic psychotherapy based on the work of an American psychologist, Carl Rogers (1902–87). It is a form of therapy in which the ideas and views of the patient, who is always called the client, are of primary importance with the therapist acting as a 'sounding board' but one who is willing to make helpful suggestions. The whole aim is to build the person's self-confidence and ability to take charge of his own development with regard to all aspects of life, including any problems such as phobias.

Visualisation therapy

It is now widely accepted that the mind exerts a great deal of influence on the health of the body. People with a cheerful, optimistic outlook on life experience better health than those who are gloomy and pessimistic. In the case of some serious illnesses, such as cancer, people who maintain a positive, 'determined-to-fight-it' attitude often do better than those who are passive, accepting or fatalistic. In these instances, life in both its extent and quality appears to be affected by the person's state of mind. It is recognised, therefore, that pictures created by the mind (as well as thoughts) can have powerful positive or negative effects on the health of the body. Those using this therapy believe that it can greatly benefit people suffering from stress, and psychological and emotional problems including phobias.

In visualisation therapy, the patient is first taught the technique of creating a mental image. A person suffering from an emotional or psychological problem, such as phobia, is asked to create a picture that is connected with the problem. The feelings created by the image are explored and discussed with the therapist and changes are made to the picture that, with time, help to resolve the problem.

This therapy is usually used alongside other techniques as part of a treatment programme. It is particularly useful with children who are naturally imaginative and find it easy to create mental pictures.

Yoga

Yoga is an Indian philosophy and way of life based on meditation, a simple, serene lifestyle and a series of exercises designed to promote spiritual, mental and physical health, harmony and a sense of wellbeing. There are various aspects and forms of yoga but the type known as *hatha* is the one usually practised in Western countries. This takes the form of a series of exercises coupled with relaxation and simple meditation that has proved beneficial to very many people.

Yoga is of particular benefit to those suffering from anxiety and stressful conditions, such as phobia, as a person usually achieves a sense of mental and physical calmness and wellbeing by carrying out the exercises and relaxation.

Yoga can be carried out as a self-help measure, either by joining a class or by carrying out exercises at home with the aid of one of the many books that are available on the subject. It may benefit a phobic person, whether or not he is undergoing other treatment, and is useful in that the person can progress at his own pace in the comfort of his own home.

Chapter 25
Psychotherapy

Psychotherapy – an introduction

A word of warning is necessary here for anyone contemplating this kind of therapy. Psychiatrists are qualified doctors, usually attached to a hospital, and people are usually referred to them by a general practitioner. A patient can, therefore, have confidence in his or her training, even if he does not get on with the actual person. This is not the case, however, with all psychotherapists.

Many psychotherapists hold a suitable professional qualification, such as a degree in psychology, and some may even be medical doctors, but there is nothing to prevent anyone setting up in business without such qualifications. Some people would argue that it is the skills of the therapist, not the qualifications, that count, but it is as well to check up on the nature of these skills first.

Most general practitioners will be able to make a recommendation. Failing this, do try to get hold of a personal recommendation from someone who has previously attended, and been satisfied with the psychotherapist. An attempt has been made to set up a register for therapists, and you could probably obtain details of this from your local library. You must feel that you can trust the person to whom you are entrusting your mind.

To some extent the skills required by the psychotherapist are those required by the successful psychiatrist. For a start, they must have good listening skills and have the ability to get people to talk about themselves, without revealing any reaction of condemnation or shock. Both need skill in interpreting what they hear from the client.

Often the problems that the clients of a psychotherapist have are not too dissimilar from those of the patients of a psychiatrist. Sometimes the difference is only one of degree. For example, two different people might feel that something is not right in their lives and might put this fact down to a bad relationship with a parent – sometimes physical or sexual abuse might be involved – but it is the extent to which this has affected the individual and what he or she decides to do about it that makes the difference.

Again, one person may become completely obsessed with a problem – something like the death of a parent, or the birth of a child may set this off. His or her mind ceases to be able to function in the way it normally does, and he or she becomes mentally ill. Medical help has to be sought, and the general practitioner recommends referral to a psychiatrist.

Another person who has much the same problem may not be mentally affected by it to nearly the same extent but may be conscious of the effect it is having on his or her life – perhaps he or she is having difficulties in forming lasting relationships. The person realises that help must be sought and thinks of psychotherapy.

The basis of modern psychoanalysis and psychotherapy goes back to the Austrian psychiatrist Sigmund Freud, the inventor of psychoanalysis. The disciplines seek to tap into the subconscious of the individual undergoing analysis or therapy and to release any hidden fears and to unblock any repressed emotions. By this means, people seek to discover more about themselves.

The major difference between psychoanalysis and psychotherapy is that, as the name suggests, the latter seeks to heal. The suppressed fears and emotions that emerge from analysis are not an end in themselves but a means by which the healing process may be begun. By unblocking the subconscious, the therapist tries to help the client towards a better understanding of himself or herself and to help him or her cope more effectively with life in the light of this understanding.

The role of the psychotherapist is to listen and interpret what the client is saying. Some people feel that simply talking to a complete stranger is, in fact, therapeutic. Friends and members of the family may be too involved, over-emotional, or condemnatory or judgmental, and are often too busy to really listen. The psychotherapist is someone who is totally uninvolved and detached, whose good opinion or otherwise does not matter, and who has time to listen.

Furthermore – and this is an important part of psychotherapy – the talking can go on over a longish period of time, often quite a few months, so that there is no sense of rush. There is plenty of time to explore past experiences and relationships. The person with a problem feels that at last there is someone there to listen and help.

The basic aim of analysis and therapy may not vary from one therapist to another, but the method of approach does. Some approaches are closer to the techniques of Freud than others and advocate that clients say anything that comes into their heads, using a kind of free association as a means of unblocking the unconscious. Other therapists may prompt the client with a few gentle leading questions, especially as a means of getting each session started.

Some adopt a more formal, traditional approach than others and ask the client to lie on a sofa in such a way that he or she is unable to see the therapist. External stimuli are reduced to a minimum in an effort to get the client to concentrate as much as possible on his or her own thoughts. Others regard this as being too rigid an approach and choose to talk to their clients in a less formal setting, although the therapists themselves are never intrusive.

Many people find psychotherapy a very useful and rewarding therapy. At the very least they can talk about things they have never dreamt of speaking about before and can learn to face up to them. They can learn to come to terms with the past and be able to reach some understanding of how the past, with its suppressed fears and emotions, has effected their present and prevented them living life to the full. People can feel much more comfortable with themselves, and be able to go forward in a much more relaxed and confident way to build a future.

A self-help programme for phobia

In recent years, some psychotherapists have turned their attention towards developing a programme of self-help measures to enable some phobic people to overcome their fear on their own. A self-help programme can help those who are determined to succeed and to whom the idea of tackling their problem in their own way and in their own time is appealing.

The programme is drawn from cognitive–behavioural measures used by psychotherapists to treat phobia but which can be adapted for use at home. There are two facets to such a programme, the first dealing with the cognitive side of phobia and the second based on exposure and overcoming fear. Several of the cognitive aspects are addressed in advance of exposure. For instance, the person starts by writing down in detail the exact nature of

281

the phobia and constructs a fear hierarchy, recording the greatest down to the least frightening situations.

All the sensations experienced during phobia are also written down and the person is instructed to rate fear on a scale of 0 to 100. The person also records his end goal or aim in relation to his particular phobia and carries this around with him and pins it up in a place where he will see it every day. In order to achieve the goal, the person may be asked to write down and learn five factors relating to his phobia.

1. Phobic fear feels horrible but is not physically harmful.
2. Phobic fear can be overcome by facing up to it.
3. The phobic situation must be encountered and not avoided for fear to be overcome.
4. The more the phobic situation is encountered, the greater grows one's self-belief in one's own ability to overcome fear.
5. Therefore, the more the phobic situation is encountered, the more fear will diminish and disappear.

In order to begin self-exposure to the phobic situation, the person may be instructed to look at a list of tactics to help him to cope. This list could include, for example, physical strategies such as simple breathing exercises or concentrating on relaxing tense muscles or mental ones such as repeating 'This feels terrible but I know that nothing is going to happen and if I stay I shall eventually feel better than I do now.'

Usually, the person is asked to choose in advance three tactics from the list that he feels will be most helpful to him and practise them at home. He is then ready to begin exposure, which should normally take place every day. After each encounter, the person should record his experiences and rate his level of anxiety on the 0 to 100 scale. By doing this each day and discussing the progress made with a trusted relative or friend, the phobic person usually finds that he is making progress and his self-confidence increases so that the whole process is reinforced.

It should be stressed that this programme may not be helpful for every phobic person, but can certainly be of benefit to some.

Chapter 26
Case Histories

Choking phobia

A youth aged sixteen years developed choking phobia after suffering a severe choking episode while eating fish. At the age of fourteen, he had lost a close friend who died as a result of choking on a piece of food and it was thought that this had influenced the onset of his own phobia.

He did not seek help until he reached the age of thirty and by this time his problem had become severe as he was only eating certain foods and had lost weight. He was treated by a form of graduated exposure therapy which involved being reintroduced to a series of foods that he had given up eating because of his phobia. Treatment was successful and he was able to eat normally thereafter.

Flying phobia

A young woman in her mid-twenties was building a successful career with a multinational company and increasingly found herself being expected to travel abroad. Unfortunately, she suffered from flight phobia and, as the condition threatened to curtail her career prospects, she decided to seek treatment.

As far as she could recall, she had always been frightened of flying but the phobia had developed following a particularly turbulent flight during childhood, when the plane on which she was travelling with her family had been diverted to another airport because of bad weather.

She was treated by graduated exposure using video material and *in vivo* trips to an airport, culminating in undertaking a short internal flight. Following this, she felt able to undertake a long-haul flight and was eventually able to overcome her phobia.

Water phobia

A middle-aged woman had a long-standing fear of taking a bath although she could manage to cope with a shower. The fear centred on sitting in a deep bath as she feared that she would somehow slip under and would not know how to get up and out and so would drown. Treatment consisted of graduated exposure to baths in which the water level was slowly increased along with challenges to the distorted beliefs that she had about bathing.

Storm phobia

An elderly woman in her mid-seventies had suffered from storm phobia since childhood, having acquired the fear as a result of being in a house that was struck by lightning and subsequently caught fire. She was treated by means of graduated exposure using audio tapes and video material featuring storms and was successfully able to overcome her phobia.

Doll phobia

A young boy, aged eleven years, had a phobia about dolls which had been present since infancy. He was successfully treated by means of graduated exposure using a series of dolls and children's model figures, ending up with ones that were quite frightening.

By the end of treatment, he was able to take a figure home with him and play with it and no longer avoided dolls in everyday life.

Balloon phobia

Balloon phobia is usually concerned with the sudden, loud noise that a balloon makes when it bursts. It is not uncommon for children to be fearful of bursting balloons, often accompanying phobia of other sudden, loud noises such as those made by fireworks, guns or thunder.

A young man aged twenty-three years had suffered from balloon phobia since early childhood when a balloon had been burst in his face at a children's party.

He was treated by flooding (exposure) therapy and was cured after three fairly intensive sessions and was thereafter able to happily enjoy social events such as parties where balloons were present.

Chapter 27
Conclusion

Phobia is a fascinating, complex and prevalent disorder, the study of which has seemed to raise as many questions as it has provided answers. Most people can probably readily sympathise with the plight of a phobic person. This is because many would admit to having a dislike, aversion or fear about something themselves, but to a lesser extent than in phobia.

However, in spite of the fact that the experience of phobia is commonplace, phobics themselves frequently go to great lengths to hide the existence of their condition and feel that it is something to be ashamed of. It is apparent that many phobics suffer acutely for years and, perhaps because of embarrassment, do not seek treatment that would be helpful to them. For any reader that is in this position, hopefully, the message of this book is that there is a great deal that can be done to relieve the phobia sufferer, ranging from self-help measures and alternative therapies to psychotherapeutic treatment programmes.

In the twenty-first century, there should no longer be any need for phobia victims to endure the miseries of this condition on their own. Hopefully, as new and greater understanding is achieved, so more and more people will find greater confidence in seeking treatment for phobia at an early stage, before the condition has a significant impact upon their life.